How To ~~Pass~~ BLITZ! ABRSM Theory
Grade 2

by Samantha Coates

Published by
Chester Music

Exclusive distributors:
Hal Leonard
7777 West Bluemound Road,
Milwaukee, WI 53213
Email: info@halleonard.com

Hal Leonard Europe Limited
42 Wigmore Street Marylebone, London, WIU 2 RY
Email: info@halleonardeurope.com

Hal Leonard Australia Pty. Ltd.
4 Lentara Court Cheltenham, Victoria, 9132 Australia
Email: info@halleonard.com.au

ISBN 978-1-78558-936-2
This book © Copyright 2017 Chester Music Limited,

For all works contained herein:
Unauthorized copying, arranging, adapting, recording,
Internet posting, public performance, or other
distribution of the music in this publication is an
infringement of copyright. Infringers are liable under the law.

A Note From the Author

Dear theory student,

Congratulations! You have just done the very best thing for your theory education — you've bought this book.

It contains more information, more revision and more worksheets than any other theory textbook (except maybe How to Blitz ABRSM Theory Grade 1!). Not only that, this edition reflects the changes in the 2018 syllabus, so it covers everything you need to know and nothing you don't!

This book follows on from the knowledge you gained in Grade 1. If you have skipped Grade 1 and you are 'jumping in' at Grade 2 level, there may be some things you need to brush up on. It's actually a great idea to work through the Grade 1 workbook before you start this book, but you should discuss this with your teacher.

Every time you see this icon:  it means there are extra resources available on the website.

Go to www.blitzbooks.com to download free worksheets, flashcards, manuscript and more!

Happy theory-ing,

Samantha

It takes more than an author and a publisher to produce a book — it takes enormous support from friends and family. Thank you to everyone who has helped me on the BlitzBooks journey, but most of all to Andrew, Thomas and Courtney... without you three, there would simply be no books.

Contents

Introducing $\frac{2}{2}$, $\frac{3}{2}$ and $\frac{4}{2}$ 6

Grouping of Rests 9

A New Sharp Key 10

Two New Flat Keys 11

Major Keys Quiz 12

Tiny Test 13

The Triplet 14

Rhythmic Revision 17

Leger Lines 18

Ten Tasks (a.k.a. 'Test') 20

Introducing $\frac{3}{8}$ 22

Time Signatures We Know 24

Timed Test 25

Major Keys Have Minor Relatives! 26

Minor Scales 28

Scale Degrees 35

Intervals 36

Quick Quiz 37

Tonic Triads 38

Terrific Triads 39

Key Signature vs Accidentals 40

Revision of Everything So Far 42

Halving and Doubling 44

Switching Clefs 48

Timed Test II 49

Box Puzzle 51

Terms and Signs 52

Yet Another Quiz 54

Word Search 58

Mad Multiple Choice 62

Test Paper... Sort Of 65

Crash Course on Grade 1 Stuff

Before we launch into Grade 2, let's revise the rhythm facts you learned in Grade 1.

Can you write the correct number of crotchet beats for each of these rhythm values?

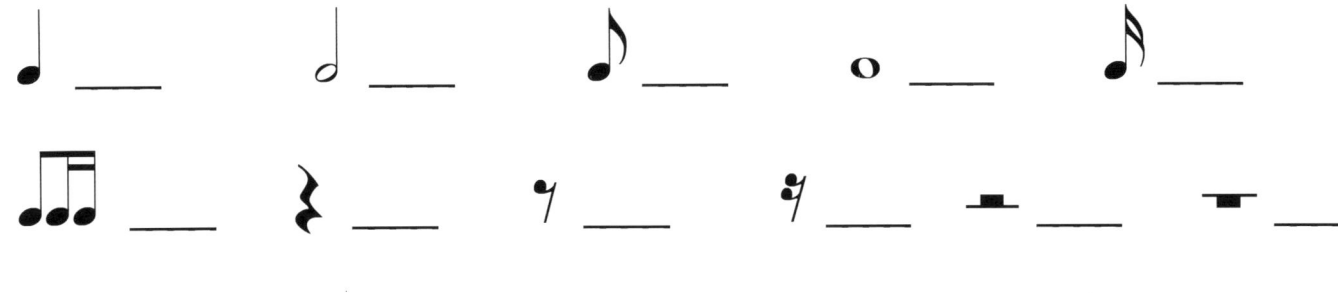

Remember the rule about dots? Of course you do. A dot adds on half the value of the note.

So ♩. = ♩ + ♩ (which equals ___ crotchet beats).

A tie, as you know, makes two notes **of the same pitch** into one sound.

Can you write a single note that would be equal to these tied notes? You might need to use dotted notes for some of them!

And now, find a way to express these single notes as two tied notes!

e.g. 𝅗𝅥 becomes ♩‿♩ or ♩.‿♪

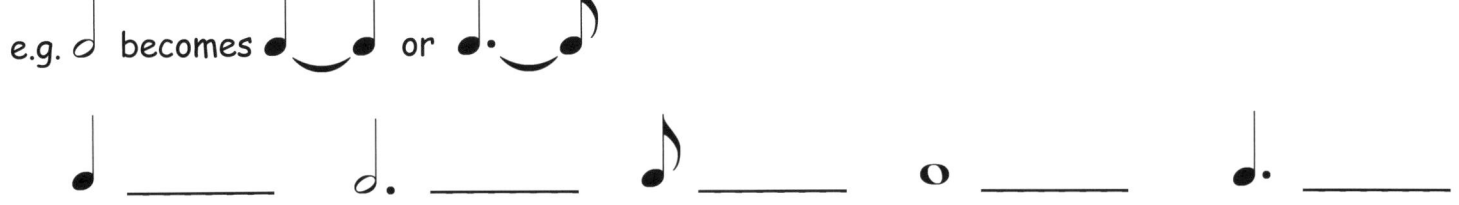

Introducing $\frac{2}{2}$, $\frac{3}{2}$ and $\frac{4}{2}$

Notice anything different about these time signatures? That's right, they have a '2' on the bottom instead of a '4'! This means that the beats are MINIM beats.

	Simple Duple	Simple Triple	Simple Quadruple
Crotchet beats	$\frac{2}{4}$ ♩ ♩	$\frac{3}{4}$ ♩ ♩ ♩	$\frac{4}{4}$ ♩ ♩ ♩ ♩
Minim beats	$\frac{2}{2}$ ♩ ♩ (same length as $\frac{4}{4}$)	$\frac{3}{2}$ ♩ ♩ ♩ (very long bar)	$\frac{4}{2}$ ♩ ♩ ♩ ♩ (super long bar)

So now you know TWO different time signatures for simple duple, triple and quadruple!

(Advance warning: we are actually going to learn about ANOTHER simple triple time signature later in this book!)

In $\frac{2}{2}$, $\frac{3}{2}$ and $\frac{4}{2}$, quavers and semiquavers are usually grouped four at a time. BUT... you can't group four together if you are crossing over two separate minim beats.

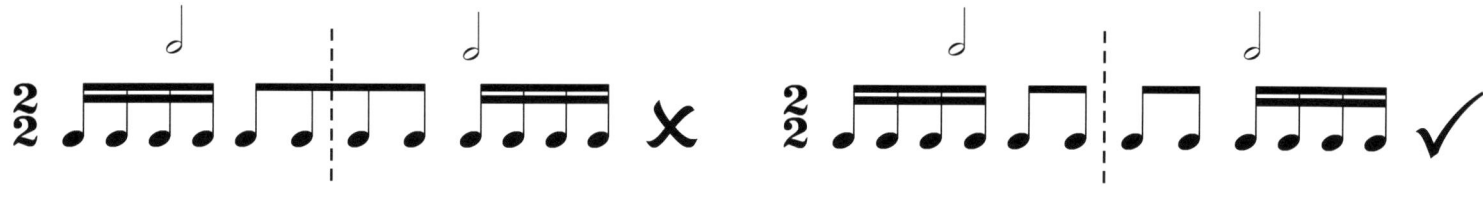

You might even see eight semiquavers grouped together, like this: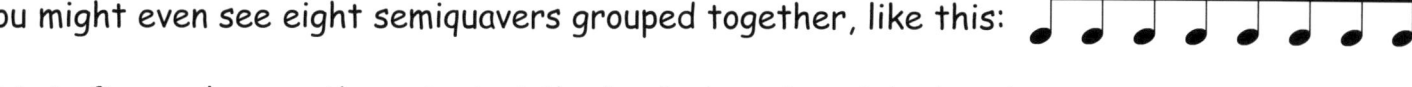

This is fine as long as they start at the beginning of a minim beat!

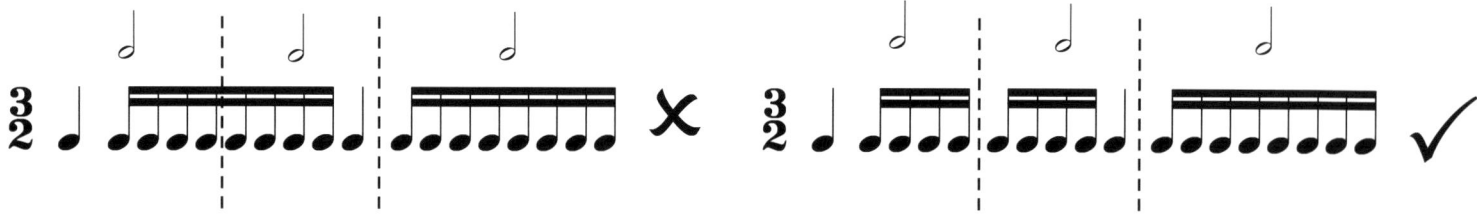

Complete these bars with quavers and semiquavers correctly grouped. Use any combinations you like, just make sure the grouping is correct.

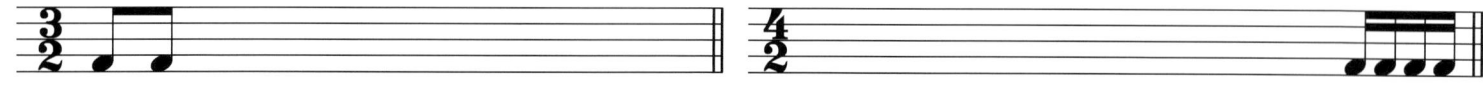

 Hot Tips on $\frac{2}{2}$

Although $\frac{2}{2}$ and $\frac{4}{4}$ look the same on paper, they really are different. Music in $\frac{2}{2}$ is usually faster than music in $\frac{4}{4}$, and a conductor would do two baton movements per bar, not four.

$\frac{2}{2}$ is also called 'cut common' time or 'alla breve'. The symbol is ₵.

Compose four bars of $\frac{2}{2}$ rhythm here:

 Hot Tips on $\frac{3}{2}$

When you are trying to identify the time signature, $\frac{3}{2}$ is easy to spot, as it has six crotchet beats in the bar. BUT... do not under any circumstances write $\frac{6}{4}$ as your answer! You must write $\frac{3}{2}$. (Just so you know, $\frac{6}{4}$ is a completely different time signature and we'll be learning about it in Grade 4!)

Compose four bars of $\frac{3}{2}$ rhythm here:

 Hot Tips on $\frac{4}{2}$

A bar of rhythm in $\frac{4}{2}$ is ridiculously easy to identify because it is SO long. But even though you'll find eight crotchet beats in the bar, **please** do not write $\frac{8}{4}$ as your answer!

Another thing about $\frac{4}{2}$... you'll see that ▬ is actually used as a half-bar rest! To write a bar of silence in $\frac{4}{2}$ you need a different kind of rest called a 'breve' rest: ▬
But don't panic, you won't be tested on this in Grade 2!

Compose four bars of $\frac{4}{2}$ rhythm here (it will be a little squishy!):

Add the Time Signature

When adding time signatures, remember that music in $\frac{2}{2}$ and $\frac{4}{4}$ looks the same. Either answer would be correct... but for now let's practise writing $\frac{2}{2}$. Also, read over the 'hot tips' on the previous page!

1. Add the correct time signatures to these rhythms:

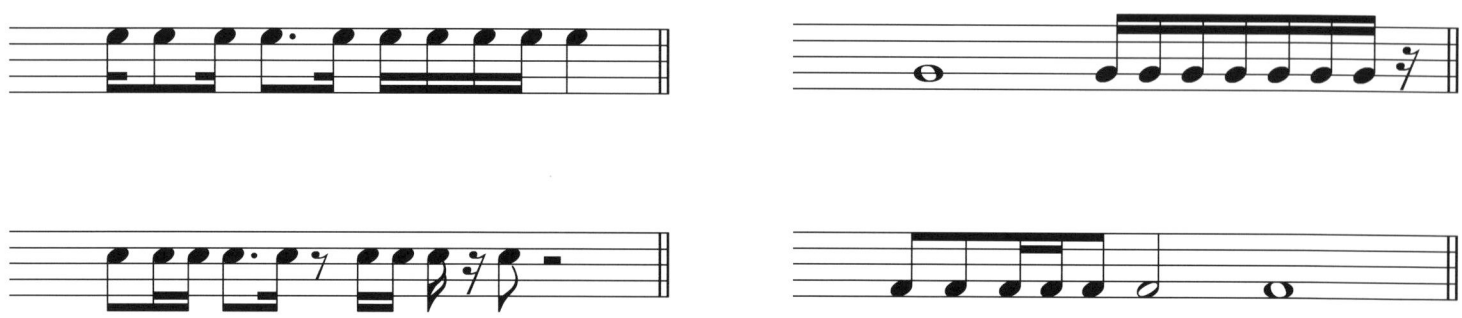

2. Add time signatures **and** the missing bar-lines to the following three melodies. The first bar-line has been done for you. Remember to add a double bar at the end!

3. Here's a tricky one... the time signature and ALL the bar-lines are missing! The big clue here is that it is meant to be four bars long. Don't forget the double bar at the end!

Grouping of Rests

Whenever you have two or more rests in a row, they must be ordered so that they complete the beat, or part of the beat, before going on to a larger rest.

For example, let's complete this bar with rests:

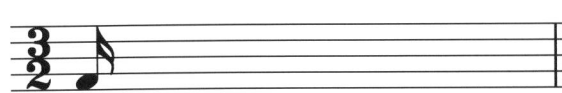

1. Always follow ♪ with 𝄾, no matter what the time signature!
2. Add 𝄾 to make it up to a crotchet beat
3. Next add 𝄽 to complete the first minim beat
4. Fill the rest of the bar with two minim rests!

Important rule: In 3/2 you may need two minim rests in a row to complete the bar. Don't be tempted to use 𝄻 instead... you may not group two minim rests together in 3/2!

Now... if you are asked to fill in rests **before** a note in the bar, just work backwards!

This semiquaver needs a 𝄾 just before it to make it up to a quaver beat, then a 𝄾 to complete the crotchet beat, then a 𝄽 to complete the minim beat. Then you can add the 𝄻 at the beginning of the bar! (Do all that now)

This bar's rests are incorrectly grouped. Rewrite it with the rests in the correct order:

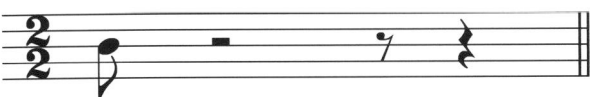
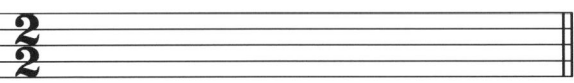

Here is a typical exam question:

'Add the correct rest/s at the places marked with an asterisk to complete each bar.'
See how it says 'rest/s'? This means even though there is only one asterisk, you might need more than one rest to complete that bar! Try this one:

Tricky! See 'important rule' above!

A New Sharp Key

Remember C, F, G and D major from Grade 1? Here are their key signatures:

There is a new sharp key in Grade 2: A major. You may have played this scale on your instrument. Its key signature looks like this:

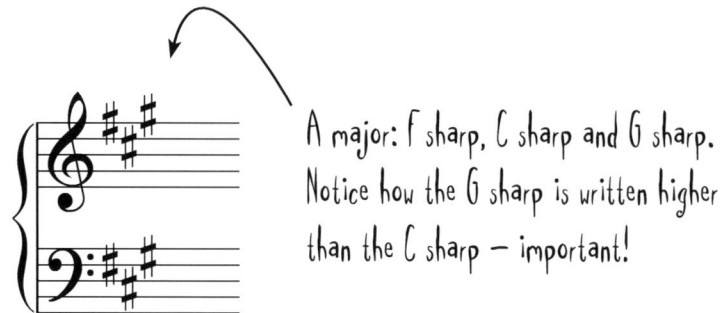

A major: F sharp, C sharp and G sharp. Notice how the G sharp is written higher than the C sharp — important!

The reason A major has this key signature is because of the patterns of tones and semitones in the scales. You probably remember from Grade 1 that the pattern is TTS TTTS. Let's look at the scale of A major:

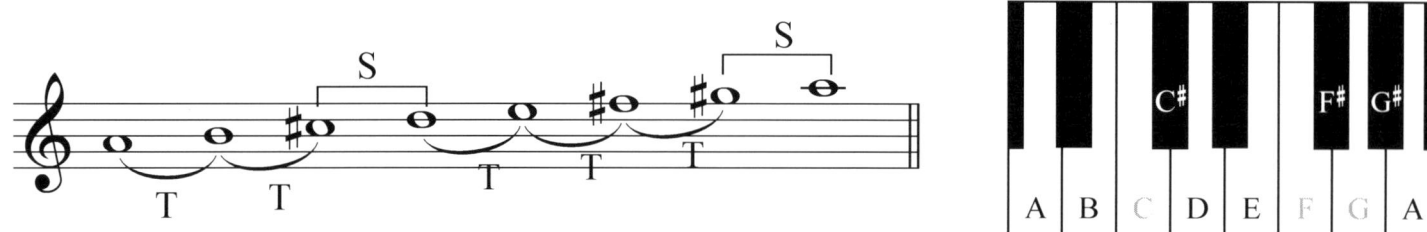

> The F, C and G must be raised, otherwise the pattern will not be correct. This is why **A major has F SHARP, C SHARP and G SHARP.**

Two New Flat Keys

There are two new major keys with **flats** in Grade 2.

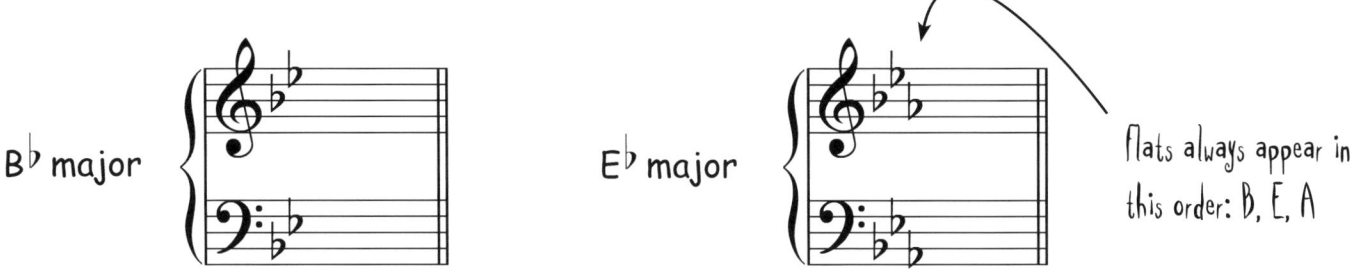

How many flats does E♭ major have? _____ How many flats in B♭ major? _____

Do the flats always appear in the same order? _____

Write these key signatures (watch out for clef changes!):

These two keys have exactly the same pattern of tones and semitones as all the other major keys we've learned so far. This means you can easily write these scales below. Write them in semibreves, and mark the semitones with square brackets.

★ B♭ major, treble clef, descending, write the key signature

★ E♭ major, bass clef, ascending, use accidentals

 DID YOU KNOW... 'How To Blitz! Key Signatures' is the perfect book to help you learn and memorise your key signatures!

11

Major Keys Quiz

1. Name three major keys that have **sharps** in the key signature. ____ , ____ and ____

2. Name three major keys that have **flats** in the key signature. ____ , ____ and ____

3. Which major key has no sharps or flats? _____

4. Write the scale of D major, using a key signature, in the bass clef. Write one octave ascending in minims.

5. In the scale you just wrote, mark the semitones with square brackets.

6. Circle the correct A major key signature (it must be correct in treble AND bass!).

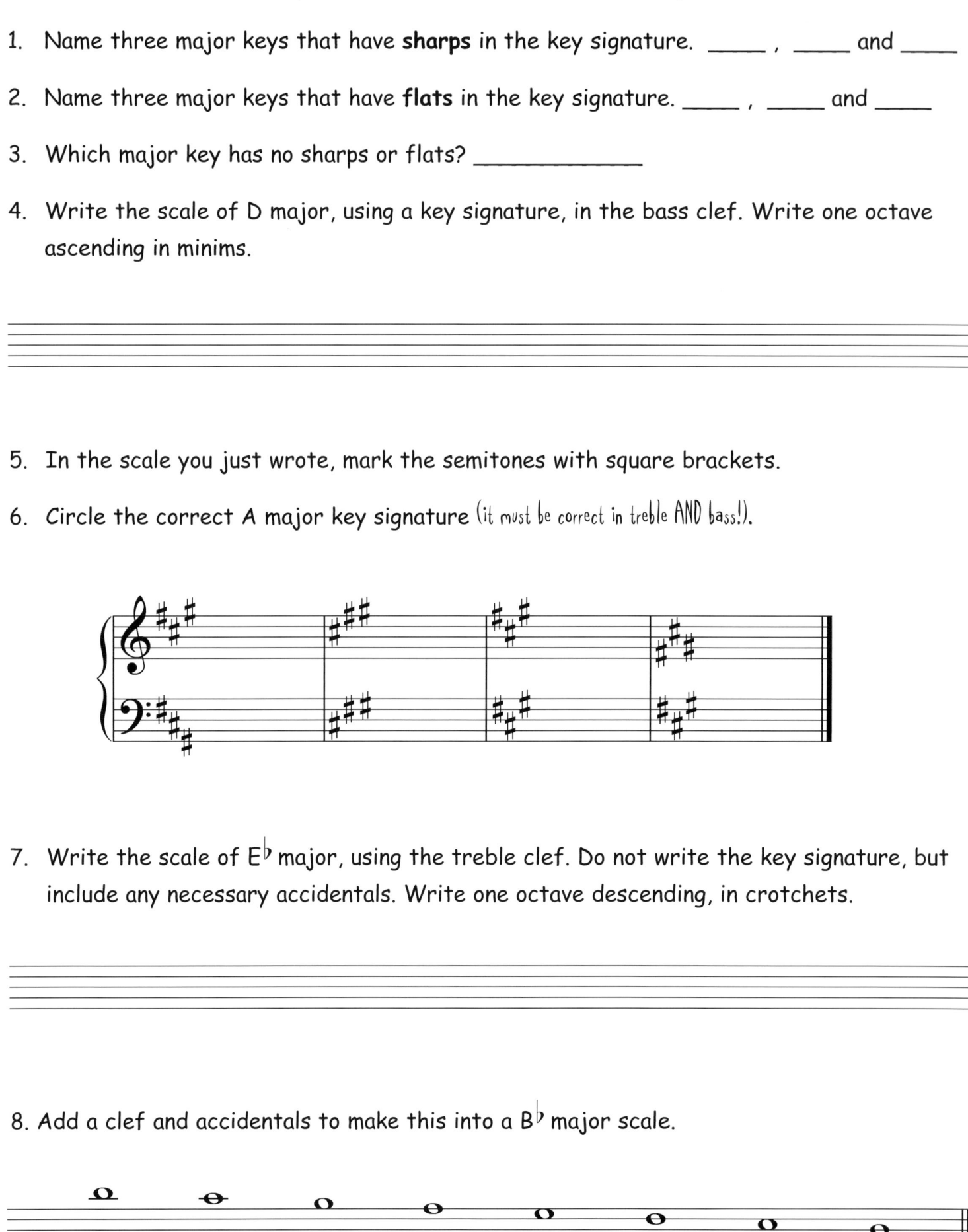

7. Write the scale of E♭ major, using the treble clef. Do not write the key signature, but include any necessary accidentals. Write one octave descending, in crotchets.

8. Add a clef and accidentals to make this into a B♭ major scale.

Tiny Test

1. Add a clef and key signature to make this melody into E♭ major. Then add the missing time signature!   /3

2. What is the time name of the longest note in the melody? _____   /1

3. Add the missing bar-lines to these melodies, then name the key of each. (Don't forget double bar-lines at the end!)   /10

Key: _____

Key: _____

4. Give the letter name of the notes marked *. Make sure you include the flat or natural sign after the letter name, depending on the key signature and accidentals.   /8

B♭ ___ ___ ___ ___ ___ ___ ___

5. How many ties are there in the melody above? _____ How many slurs? _____   /2

6. Rewrite these notes in order from **longest** to **shortest**.   /6

♪ o 𝅗𝅥. 𝅗𝅥 𝅘𝅥. ♪   ___ ___ ___ ___ ___ ___

Total: /30

The Triplet

A quaver triplet looks like this ♩♩♩ or this ♩♩♩ . It is equal to one crotchet beat.

The formal definition of a triplet is:

'Three notes played in the time of two notes of equal value' (learn this!)

So ♩♩♩ = ♩♩ = ♩ = 1

A triplet ALWAYS has a number '3' on the top or the bottom of the group of quavers, otherwise this grouping would be incorrect. If there is no number '3', then it's not a triplet!

Fill the following bars with quaver triplets: (don't forget the number '3')

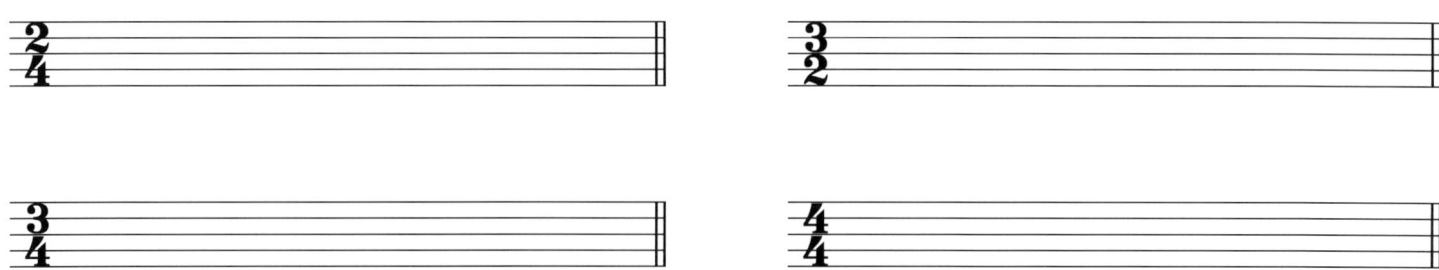

Insert the correct time signature to each of these complete bars:

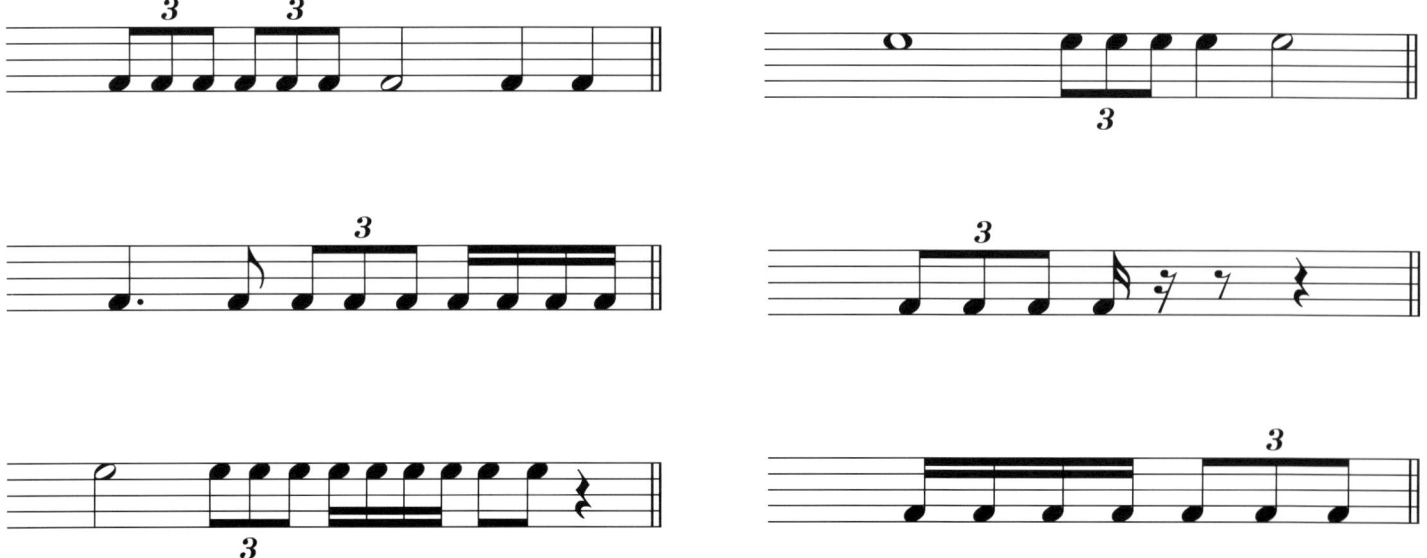

More Triplets

The thing is, there are actually LOADS of different types of triplets, not just quaver triplets like we did on the previous page.

Crotchet and minim triplets are not connected by a beam, so in the table below you'll need to draw the bracket connecting the notes, with the '3' over/under the middle note.

Take any two note values	Make them into a triplet by adding another note and popping a '3' on them	The value stays the same. Now use the triplets in a rhythm!
♩ ♩	3 ♩ ♩ ♩	4/4 [rhythm with triplet]
𝅗𝅥 𝅗𝅥	3 𝅗𝅥 𝅗𝅥 𝅗𝅥	4/2
♫	3 ♪♪♪	2/4

The following rhythm looks as though it has wrong grouping and incorrect beats... that's because the triplet signs are missing! Add them in, then try clapping it (which is quite tricky!).

Add time signatures to these complete bars:

Compose your own two-bar rhythm here, using as many types of triplets as you can!

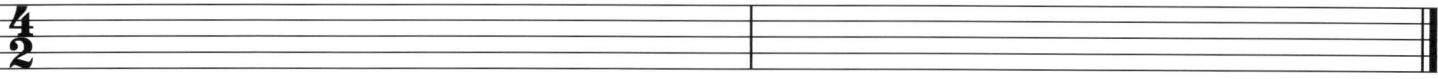

That's a lot of notes, eh?

Even More Triplets (when will it stop?)

Triplets don't always contain just notes. Sometimes you get RESTS inside a triplet (gasp).

So instead of  you might see

If the rest comes at the beginning, you'll see a beam AND a bracket:

Also, instead of 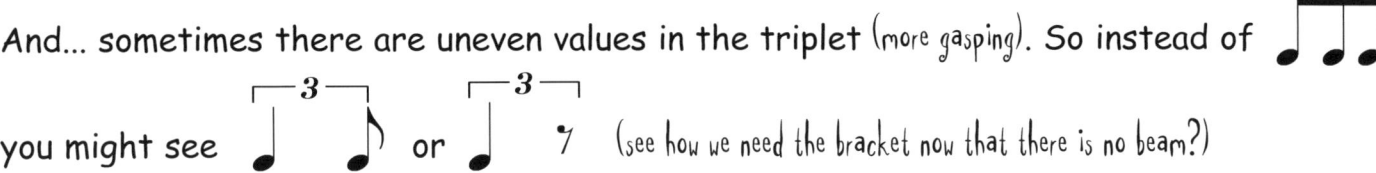 you might see

And... sometimes there are uneven values in the triplet (more gasping). So instead of

you might see   or   (see how we need the bracket now that there is no beam?)

Add the missing rests to this rhythm with triplets:

And now, for your last trick... add the correct time signature to these complete bars:

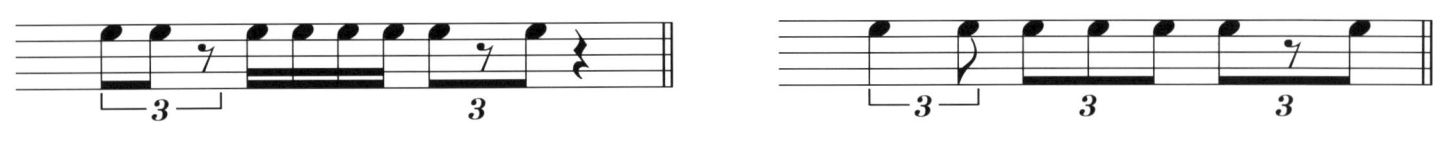

Good work!

If you have ever played any jazzy pieces, you might have seen this instruction:

This tells you to play in a 'long-short' rhythm instead of even quavers, which is known as a 'swing' rhythm. Now you understand the theory behind it!

Rhythmic Revision

Figure out how many beats are missing from each of these bars. Then complete each one using any sort of triplets you want! Use a combination of notes and rests.

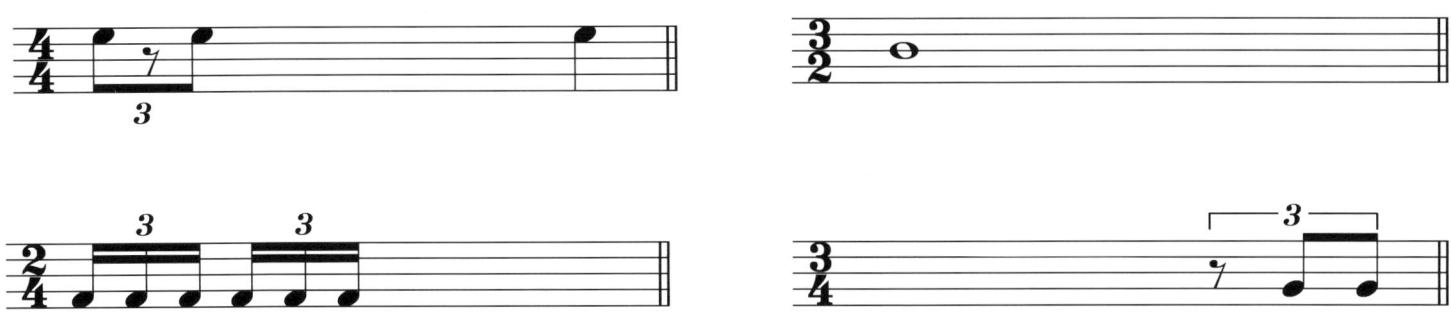

How many different ways can you think of writing one crotchet beat? Write them all in this box. Some ideas are there to start you off...

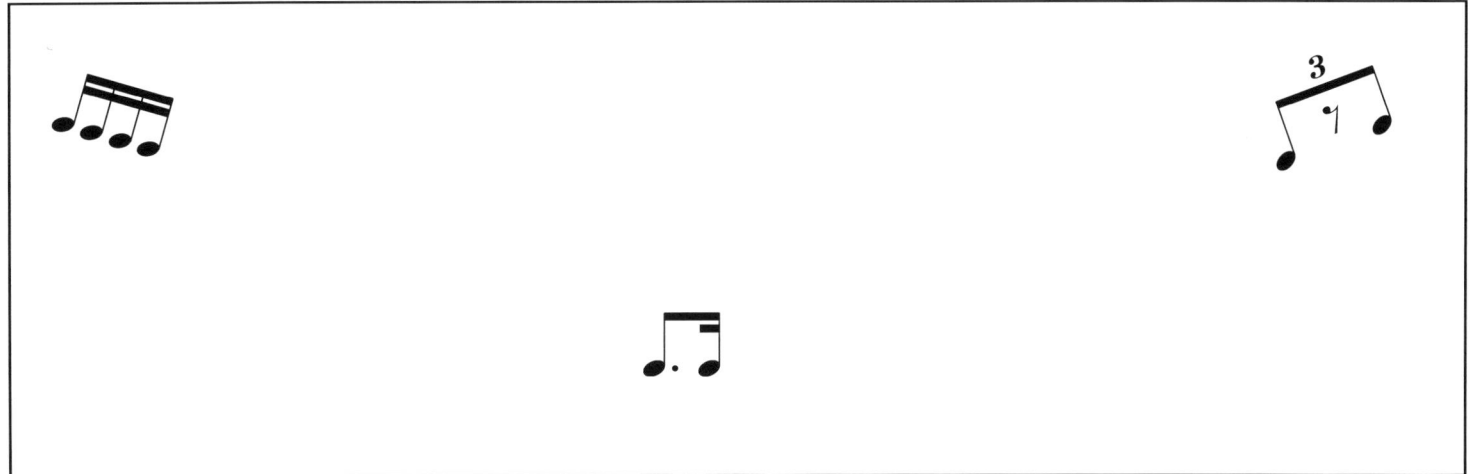

Add time signatures and the missing bar-lines to these melodies (including double bars, of course!):

Leger Lines

In Grade 2 we need to work with notes that are up to TWO leger lines above or below the stave, but of course there's actually no limit to how many you can use in general music!

Wow! What note is THAT???

All of these notes are referred to as notes 'above' or 'below' the treble stave. (The notes in grey are not leger line notes, obviously, but they are also referred to as 'D below the stave' etc.)

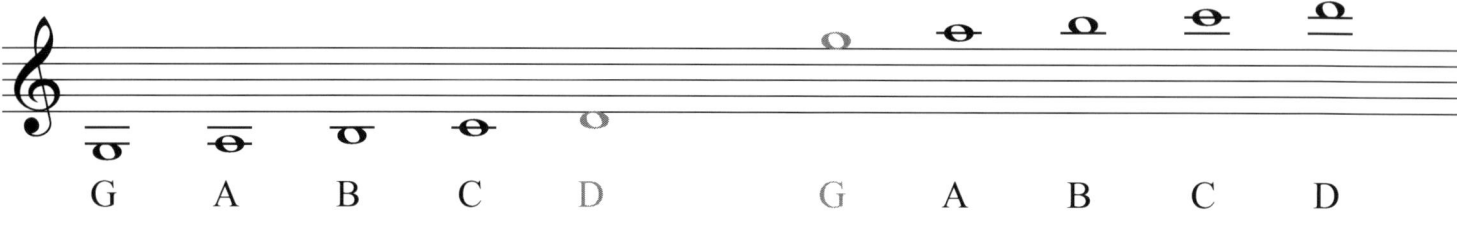

G A B C D   G A B C D

And now here are the bass notes that live 'above' or 'below' the stave:

B C D E F   B C D E F

Sometimes you'll need to draw notes with accidentals on leger lines. The width of the leger line does not change.

The sharp does NOT need its own leger line! It sort of hangs in the air, in line with the note.

By the way, what note is this? _____

Remember to keep leger lines spaced the same distance apart as the staff lines. Draw the line or lines first, then draw the note, then the accidental! Trace these then draw your own, including accidentals of your choice...

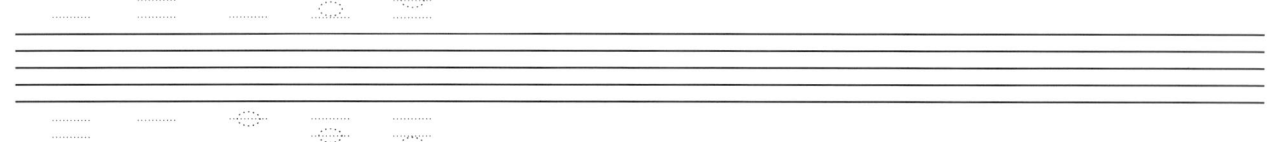

More To Do With Leger Lines

Remember this from Grade 1: $8^{va}\text{-------}\rceil$? It means to play an octave higher than written.

So  actually sounds like this

You can also place '8va' underneath notes to indicate an octave lower, but the more correct sign for this is $8^{vb}\text{------}\rfloor$ which stands for 'ottava bassa' ('at the octave **below**').

Rewrite these notes at their sounding pitch. You'll need to use lots of leger lines, of course!

 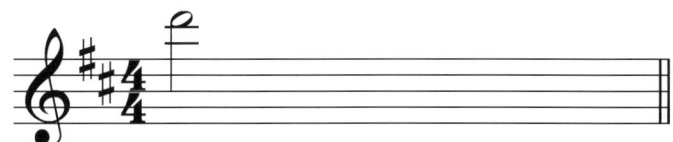

 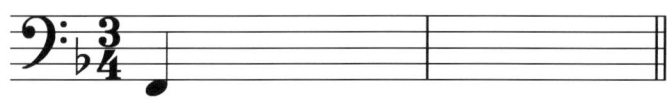

You can get rid of leger lines by changing clef:

Write the equivalent sounding note for these. You won't need leger lines in your answers!

 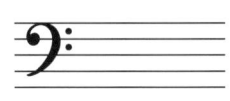  

Try rewriting this short melody in the treble clef. Follow the shape exactly and keep the rhythm the same. The only thing you'll need to change is the direction of the stems.

 DID YOU KNOW... reading music with lots of leger lines can be really annoying, so composers often change clefs or use the 8va sign. Isn't that so nice of them???

Ten Tasks (a.k.a. 'Test')

1. Here is a melody in B♭ major (although it doesn't look quite right, does it?). Do all the things listed below to make the melody complete!

   ★ Add the correct clef
   ★ Add the key signature
   ★ Add a triplet sign to the quavers at the beginning of bar 2
   ★ Add the time signature and missing bar-lines
   ★ Draw a circle around the lowest note
   ★ Draw a square around the shortest note
   ★ Add a tie in an appropriate place

   There! It's done. Now play it or get someone to play it for you!

2. Rewrite this melody with correct grouping/beaming of the notes.

3. Name these notes.

   _____ _____ _____ _____ _____

4. Circle the note in question 3 which is the 5th scale degree of E♭ major.

5. Name these scales.

Scale: _____

Scale: _____

6. Figure out where the triplet signs should go in order to make these rhythms correct:

7. Add a clef and accidentals to make this the scale of B♭ major.

Now make all the notes into minims!

8. How many planets are there in the solar system? _____ (Not essential Grade 2 knowledge)

9. Add the correct rest/s at the places marked * to complete each bar. Tricky!

10. How many semiquavers are there in a dotted semibreve? (Hint: LOTS) _____

✓ Well done on completing all 10 tasks! Now go back and check all your work.

Introducing 3/8

For the first time, we have the number '8' on the bottom! The '8' means quaver beats.

Therefore, 3/8 means three QUAVER beats per bar, **simple triple**.

It's just like 3/4 but with quavers instead of crotchets!

3/4 = ♩ ♩ ♩ = three crotchet beats per bar = simple triple

3/8 = ♪ ♪ ♪ = three quaver beats per bar = simple triple

You will usually see all the quavers in the bar grouped together like this: ♫♪
This is quite OK... 3/8 is the only time signature in Grade 2 where a group of three quavers is allowed without a triplet sign!

There are lots of possible groupings of quavers and semiquavers. It's also quite common to see dotted quavers and semiquaver triplets. Check out this melody:

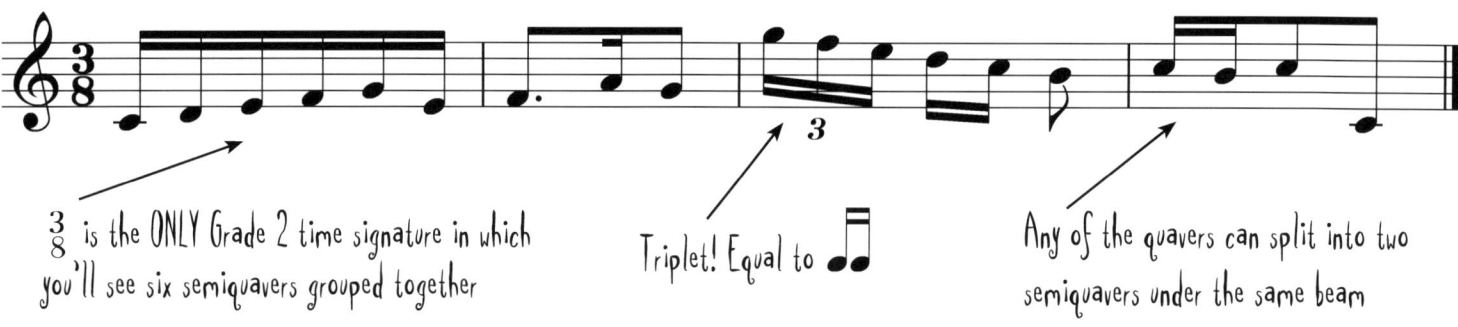

3/8 is the ONLY Grade 2 time signature in which you'll see six semiquavers grouped together

Triplet! Equal to ♫

Any of the quavers can split into two semiquavers under the same beam

Rests in 3/8 should be kept separate (just like 3/4 and 3/2).

3/8 ♪ 𝄾 𝄾   is correct, however   3/8 ♪ 𝄽   is not!

Complete each of these bars with quavers and semiquavers correctly grouped.

Short Quiz on 3/8

1. Add the correct rest/s at each place marked with an asterisk. Remember, you may need to write more than one rest!

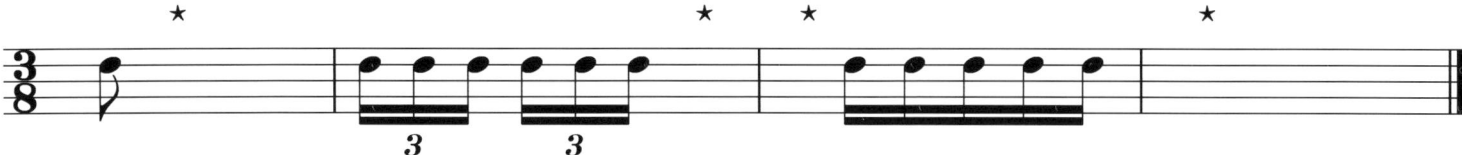

2. Did you remember to use a whole-bar rest in the last bar above? Yes/No (If not, fix this now)

3. Complete these bars as directed

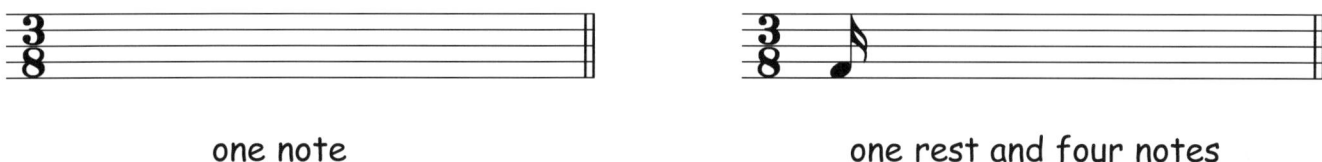

       one note   one rest and four notes

4. Add the bar-lines and time signature to this melody. (You can probably guess what the time signature is, given the title of this page)

5. Name the key of the melody above: _____

6. What does the '8' mean in the time signature of 3/8? _____

7. Look back at the the melody in question 4. If you were to double the value of all the notes and rests, the new time signature would be 3/4. It would look like this (see if you can finish it off):

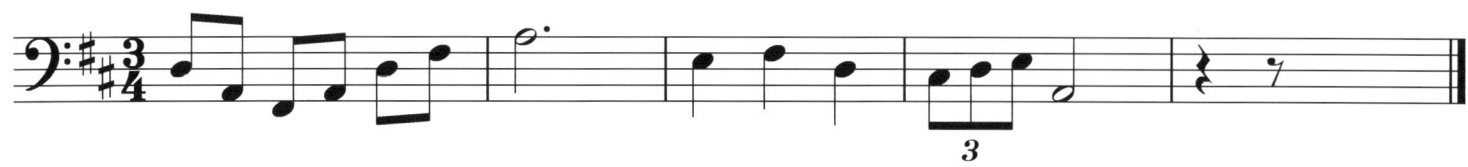

8. If you doubled the note values AGAIN, what time signature would you get? _____

Time Signatures We Know

Write the definitions of each of the time signatures below (e.g. simple duple). Then compose two bars of really creative rhythm with correct grouping of notes and rests!
(Don't use too many minims or semibreves — make it interesting!)

Time sig	Definition	Compose two bars of interesting rhythm
2/4		
3/4		
4/4 or C		
2/2 or ₵		
3/2		
3/8		
4/2		

Once you've finished writing your rhythms, clap them to your teacher. Then choose your favourite rhythm and extend it by another two bars... and write it down here!

Timed Test

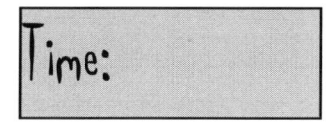

Time yourself doing this page. Do it as fast as you can, then record your finishing time above. But... guess what? Your teacher will **ADD ON 10 SECONDS** for every mistake you make! It's fun to go fast, but it's more important to be **accurate**. Start the clock!

1. How many quavers are there in this note? o• _____

2. What is the definition of a triplet? _____

3. Name these major key signatures.

_____   _____   _____   _____

4. Complete this bar with rests: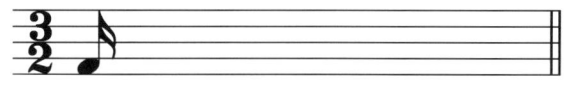

5. Name these notes, then rewrite them one octave higher, using leger lines.

   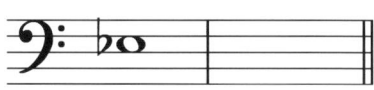   

_____   _____   _____

6. Who wrote Beethoven's 5th symphony? _____

STOP THE CLOCK – FILL IN YOUR TIME AT THE TOP!

After marking this with your teacher, tick one of the following:

☐ I made no mistakes! I keep my time of _____ !

☐ I made _____ mistakes. My new time is _____ .

25

Major Keys Have Minor Relatives!

There is a minor key that has the same key signature as C major. It is A minor. This means that C major and A minor are **related** – sort of like brother and sister! Write the key signature of C major and A minor here: (ridiculously easy)

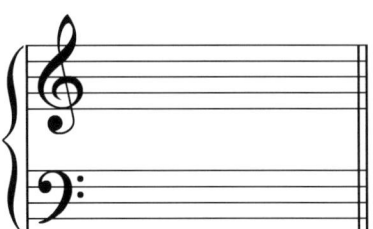
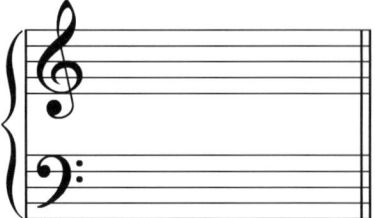

C major   A minor

★ **Can you think of a word beginning with C and ending with A?** _____ ★

G major also has a relative minor – E minor. This means that G major and E minor both have the same key signature. Write them here, in both treble and bass clefs:

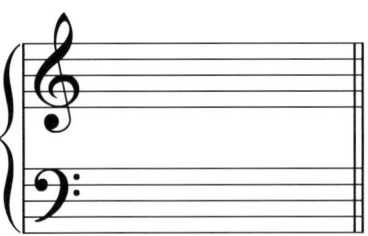
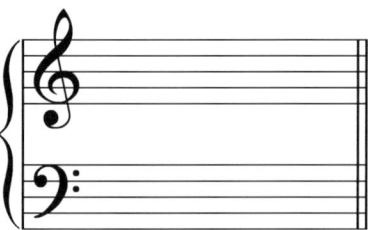

G major   E minor

★ **Can you think of a word beginning with G and ending with E?** _____ ★

Finally, F major's relative minor is D minor. You guessed it... their key signatures are exactly the same. Write them here:

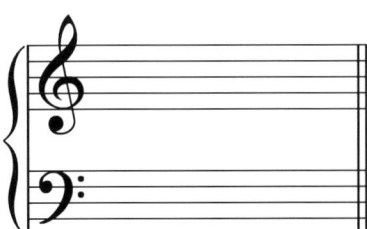
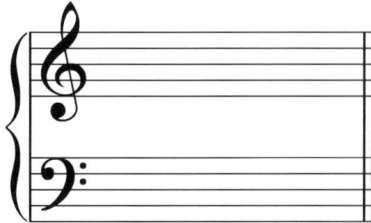

F major   D minor

★ **Can you think of a word beginning with F and ending with D?** _____ ★

Remembering Relatives

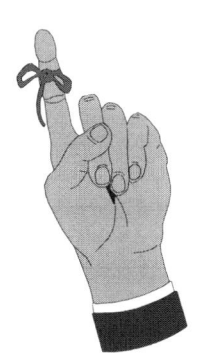

The words you chose on the previous page will help you to remember which keys are related to which. (The first letter of your word is for the major key and the last letter is for the minor key!) Write your words and key signatures into this grid:

Relatives	Word to remember relatives	Key signature of these keys
C major is related to **A minor**		
G major is related to **E minor**		
F major is related to **D minor**		

So now you know LOTS of key signatures! Let's practise some (watch out for clef changes):

E♭ major   A minor   D minor   A major   B♭ major

E minor   D major   D minor   B♭ major   G major

Minor Scales

Now that you know the three minor key signatures of A, E and D minor, it's time to learn about scales in those keys.

There are actually THREE types of minor scale:

NATURAL MINOR: Exactly the same notes as the relative major scale, but starting three semitones lower. Since there are no changes it is named 'natural'. Here is the scale of A natural minor:

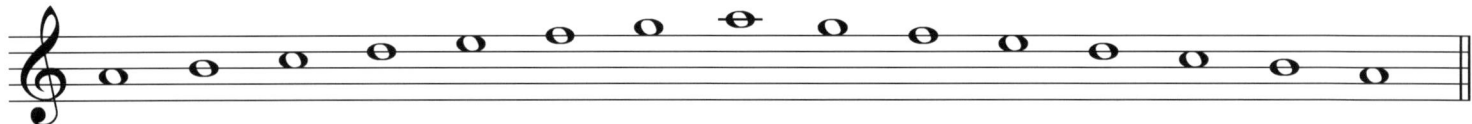

HARMONIC MINOR: The same notes as the natural minor scale but with a raised 7th note. The raised 7th makes it easy to harmonise (i.e. to add chords), which is why it is called 'harmonic'. Here is A harmonic minor:

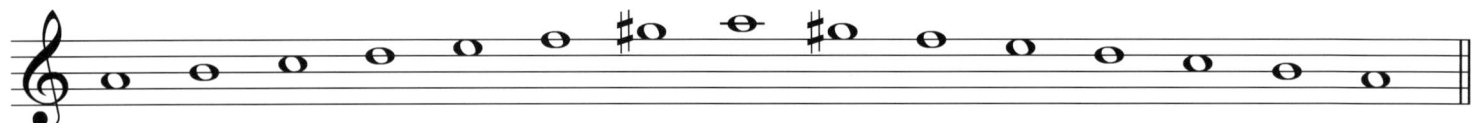

MELODIC MINOR: Sort of a combination of the above: raised 6th AND 7th on the way up, and natural minor on the way down! (How very complicated!) This form is much easier to sing, which is why it is called 'melodic'. You guessed it... here is A melodic minor:

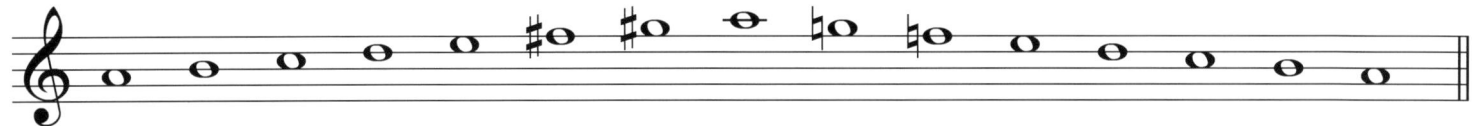

In your exam you won't be tested on natural minor, but you'll have to write EITHER harmonic OR melodic minor scales. Yes, you actually get to choose! (However, you'll be so good at both forms by the time you have finished this book that choosing will be difficult!)

DID YOU KNOW... the natural minor scale is also known as the Aeolian mode. Discuss this more with your teacher!

Harmonic Minor Scales

Since you know the key signatures of three minor keys, writing harmonic minor scales in those keys will be easy!

Write the scale of A harmonic minor:
- ★ use a key signature
- ★ write one octave ascending
- ★ use semibreves

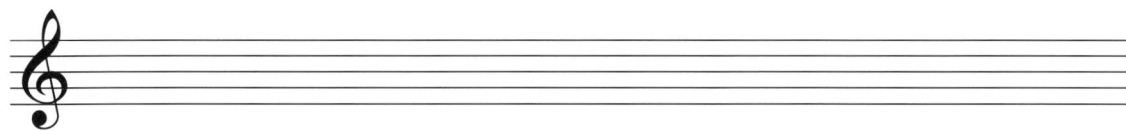

Good work! But guess what? The scale is not finished yet! As you learned on the previous page, in harmonic minor scales you must **RAISE THE 7ᵀᴴ NOTE!**

Now, which sign is used to **raise** the pitch of a note? Sharp / Flat (circle correct answer)

So now find the 7th note of your scale and draw a _____ sign just before it!

Write the scale of D harmonic minor:
- ★ use accidentals
- ★ write one octave going down
- ★ use semibreves

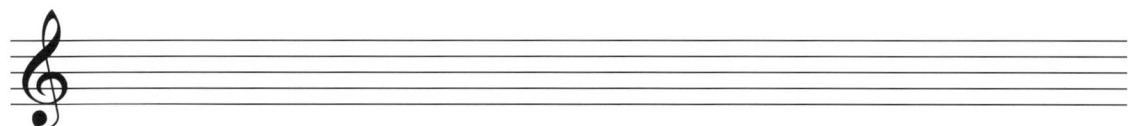

Have you added an accidental instead of the key signature of D minor? Yes / No

Did you **also** remember to raise the 7th note? Yes / No (And did you count up from the lowest note? Yes / No)

Great job! Just remember: when writing minor scales with accidentals, you ALSO need an accidental for the raised 7th!

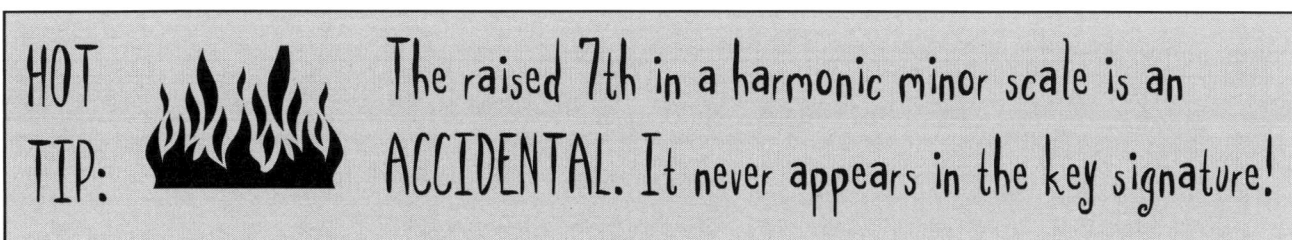

Melodic Minor Scales

Play some melodic minor scales on your instrument, or ask your teacher to play some for you. You can hear the changes ascending and descending: that's because we **raise** the 6th and 7th degrees on the way up, and **lower** them both on the way down.

Try adding the correct accidentals to this A melodic minor scale:

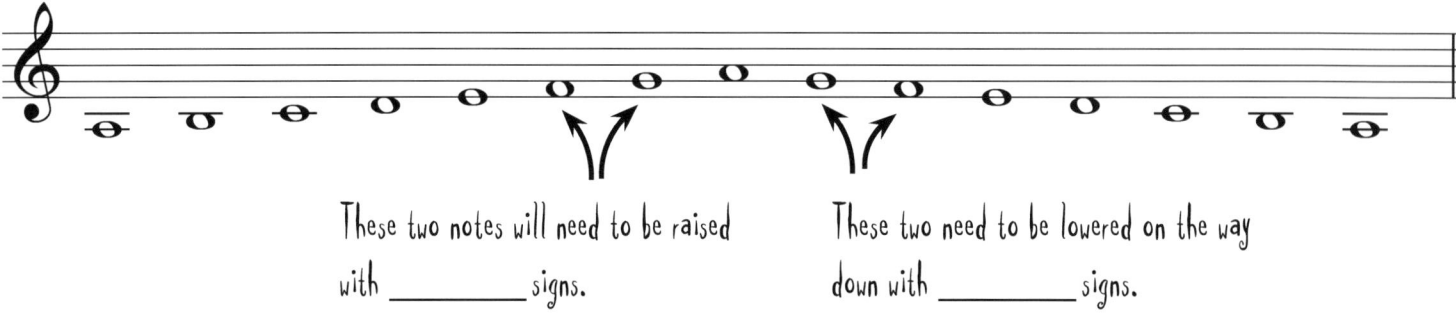

These two notes will need to be raised with _____ signs.

These two need to be lowered on the way down with _____ signs.

The D melodic minor scale is a bit trickier, because we need to use a natural sign as well as a sharp on the way up, and a flat sign as well as a natural on the way down!

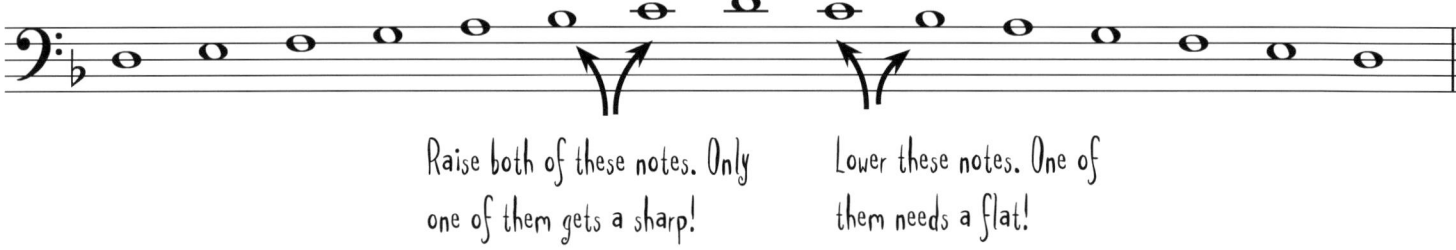

Raise both of these notes. Only one of them gets a sharp!

Lower these notes. One of them needs a flat!

Another interesting fact about melodic minors: if you are asked to write the descending form only, you don't need any natural signs. In fact, if there is a key signature you won't need any accidentals at all! Here's E melodic minor descending:

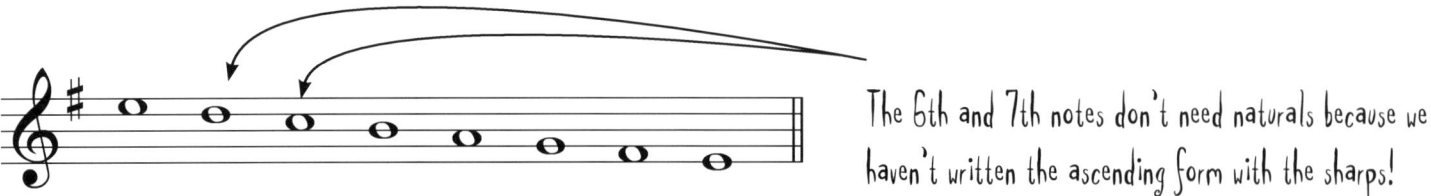

The 6th and 7th notes don't need naturals because we haven't written the ascending form with the sharps!

 INTERESTING FACT: The melodic minor is literally more 'melodic' because it gets rid of the three-semitone gap (called an 'augmented 2nd') between scale degrees 6 and 7 of the harmonic minor scale, which is a very awkward interval in melodies. We'll discuss this further when we do melody writing in later grades!

Awesome Accidentals

Add accidentals to make the following scales correct, then add a double bar-line.

(harmonic minor)

(melodic minor)

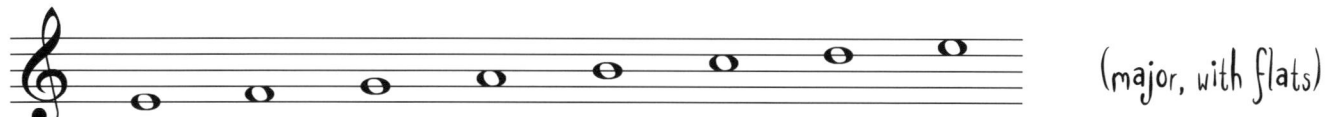
(major, with flats)

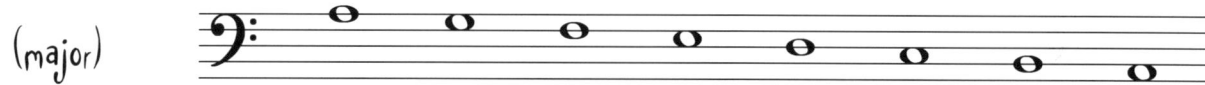
(major)

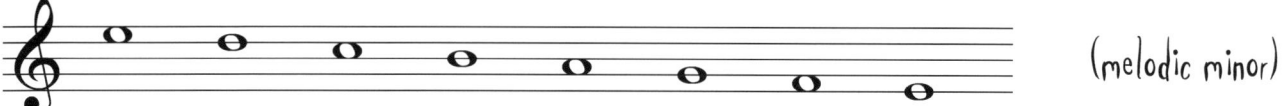
(melodic minor)

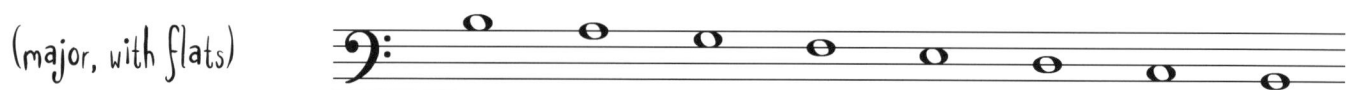
(major, with flats)

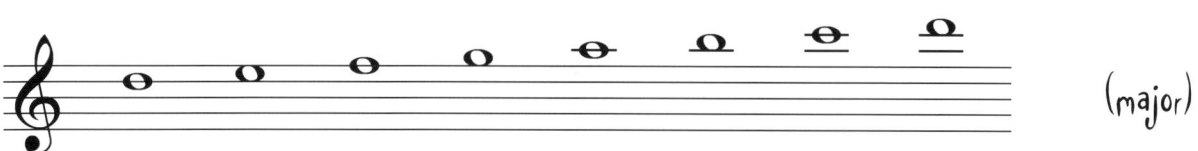
(major)

Add a clef and any accidentals required to make this into a D melodic minor scale

Have you placed all of your accidentals BEFORE the notes?

All About Scales

1. Write an A melodic minor scale ascending and descending. Use a key signature, but add all the necessary accidentals! Write the scale in minims.

2. Is the following minor scale harmonic or melodic? _____

3. Name these notes. They all come from the key of A major/A minor (circle correct answer).

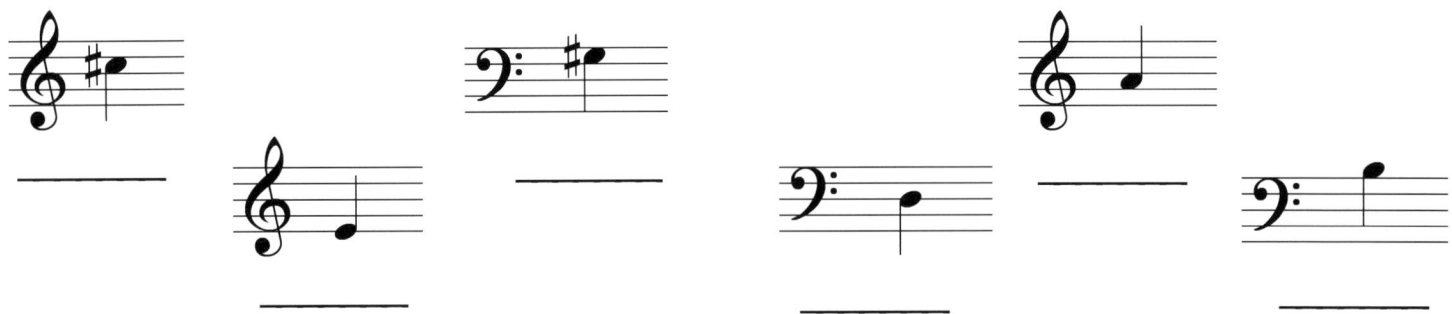

5. Write these key signatures (watch out for clef changes!).

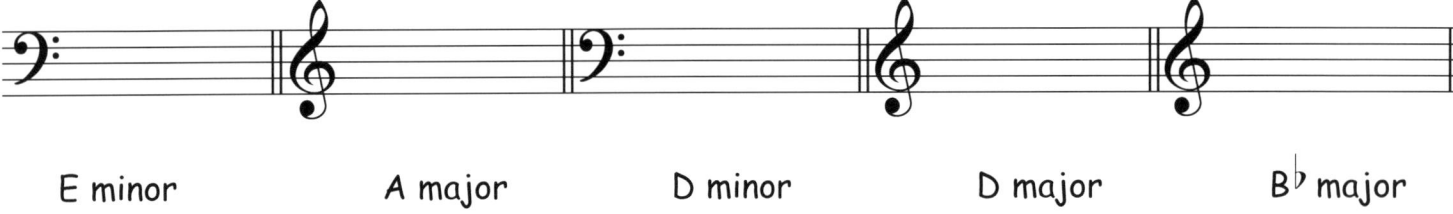

  E minor   A major   D minor   D major   B♭ major

6. Add the correct clef and any necessary sharp, flat or natural signs to each of the named scales below. Do NOT add key signatures.

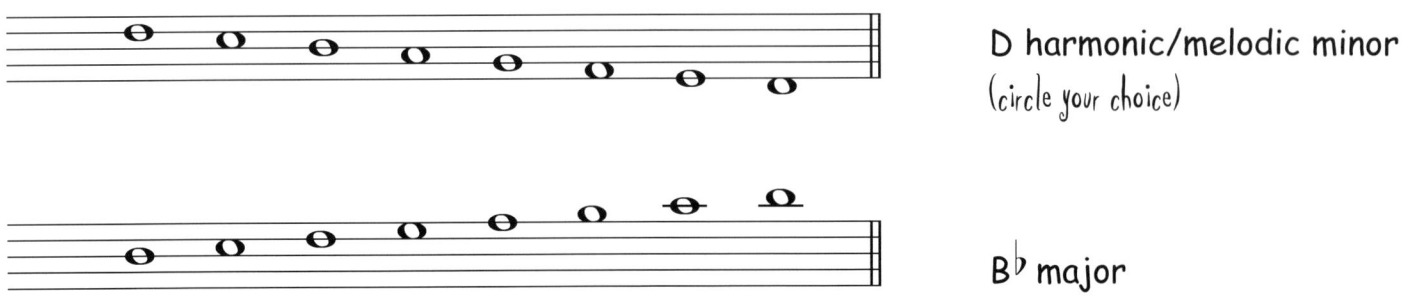

D harmonic/melodic minor (circle your choice)

B♭ major

Major or Minor?

It's really important to be able to work out the key of a written melody. There are three clues that will help you find your answer:

1. The key signature – this could represent major or minor (revise 'Remembering Relatives' on page 27).
2. The last note – melodies usually end on scale degree no. 1, the 'tonic';
3. Accidentals (warning: a melody may still be in a minor key even if there are no accidentals — check the last note).

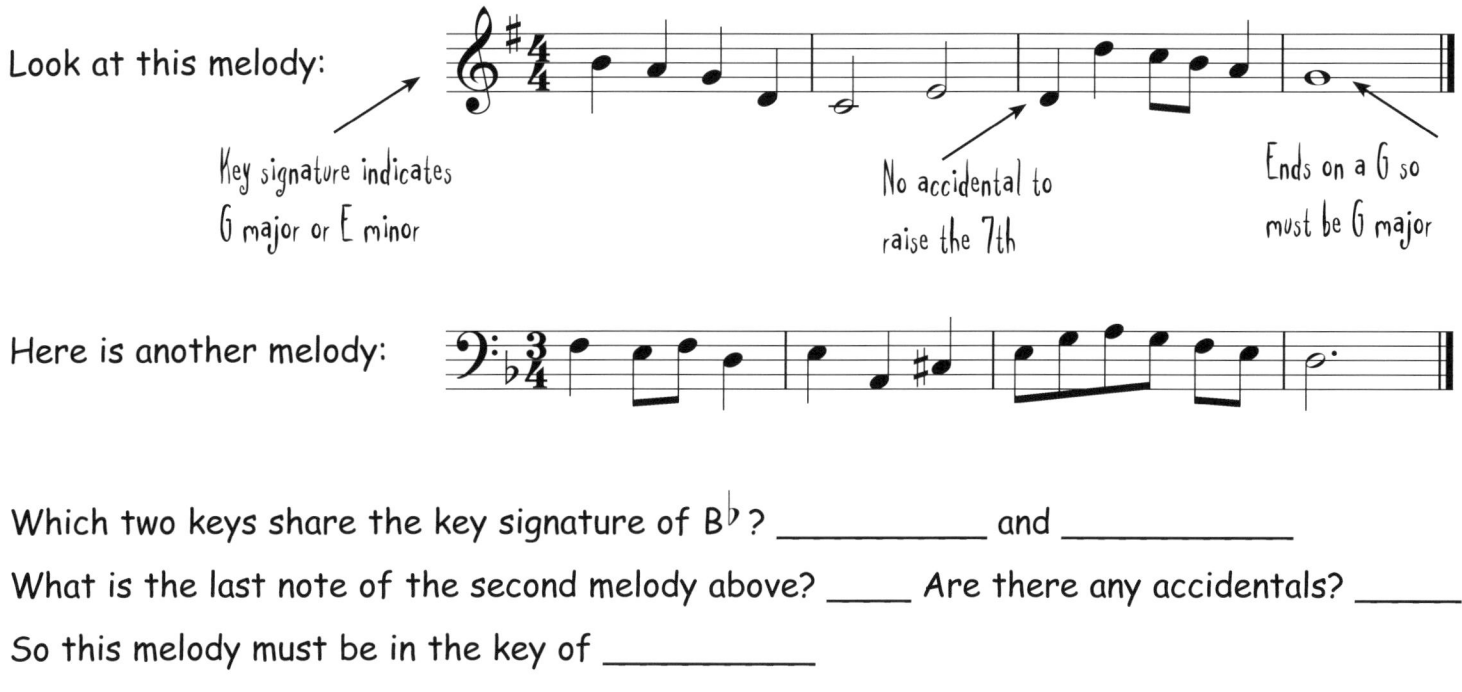

Look at this melody:
Key signature indicates G major or E minor
No accidental to raise the 7th
Ends on a G so must be G major

Here is another melody:

Which two keys share the key signature of B♭? _____ and _____

What is the last note of the second melody above? _____ Are there any accidentals? _____

So this melody must be in the key of _____

Name the key of these short melodies. Remember your three clues, and **check the clef**!

Key: _____

Key: _____

Key: _____

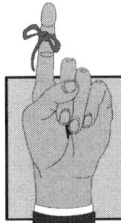

IMPORTANT: Melodies in minor keys are just called 'minor'. Only scales are referred to as 'melodic minor' or 'harmonic minor'!

Name These Keys

☐ Clef checked

☐ Key signature checked

☐ Last note checked

☐ Accidentals checked (Warning: a melody that has no accidentals could still be in a minor key! Always check the last note.)

Scale Degrees

Writing the scale degrees in a melody is easy – you did lots of this in Grade 1! All you need to do is work out the key (which is sometimes told to you, yay!) and **count**.

The following melody is in _____ major. Fill in the missing scale degrees:

     5th   ___   ___   ___ ___   ___   ___

Notice how that melody did not start on the 1st degree of the scale (the 'tonic')? This happens a lot – do not assume the first note of a melody is scale degree no. 1!

Now go back to the previous page and write the scale degrees under all those melodies!

Another type of task you'll come across in your exam is this: you are given a set of individual notes, and you have to work out which key they all belong to. You have to look carefully at which notes do and do not have accidentals:

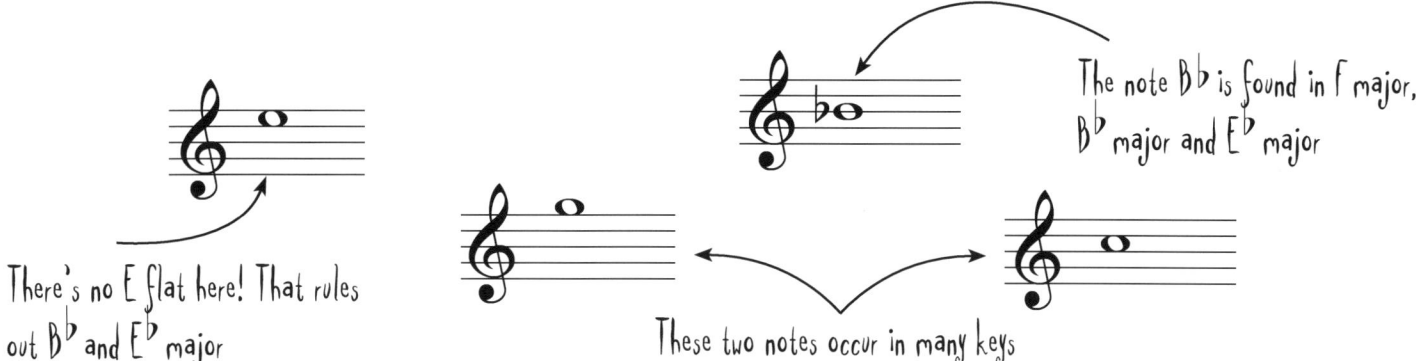

So, taking into account the accidentals, the four notes above must all be from the key of _____. Good work!

Name the key of these sets of notes:

                                                 = _____ major

                                                = _____ major

Intervals

Intervals in Grade 2 are just the same as Grade 1 – easy! Some quick revision points:

★ The **lower** note is the tonic (no. 1); just count up to find the name of the interval.
★ 'Harmonic' intervals are written vertically, like a chord.
★ 'Melodic' intervals are written side by side, like a melody.

Write the following melodic intervals. Remember to write your note **next to** the given note!

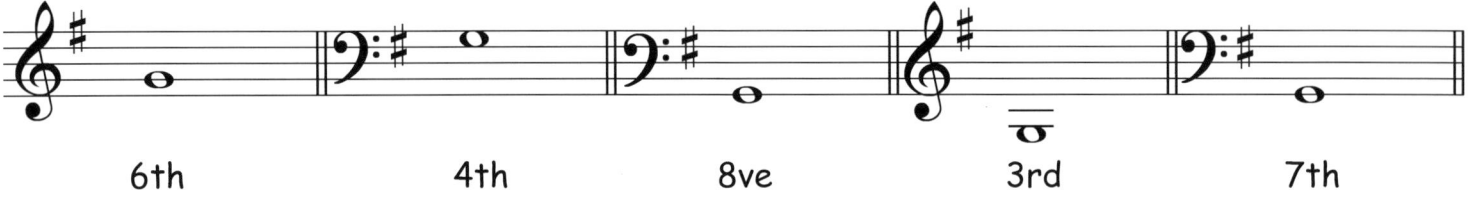

      6th   4th   8ve   3rd   7th

In what key are all of the above intervals? _____

If the given tonic note is very high, you will need to use leger lines to draw your intervals. Trace these intervals with leger lines, then name each interval.

Hint: for notes on leger lines, trace the line first, then the note!

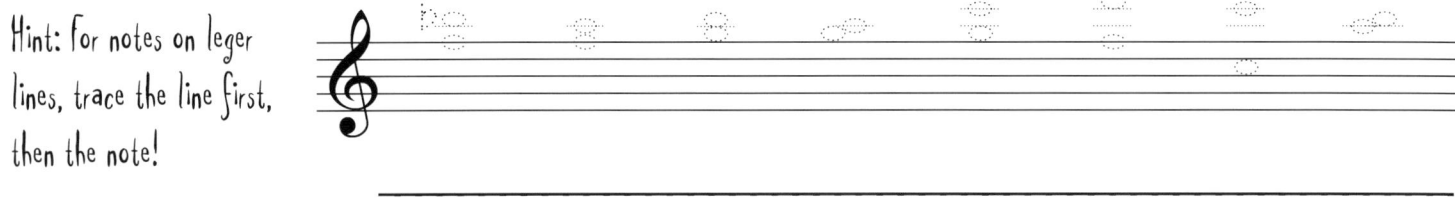

_____

Write these harmonic intervals **above** the given tonic notes (yes, you'll have to use leger lines):

      5th   6th   4th   3rd   5th   2nd

These melodic intervals have the lower note as the SECOND note! It doesn't matter... the lowest note is always no. 1. Name these (they are all in A major):

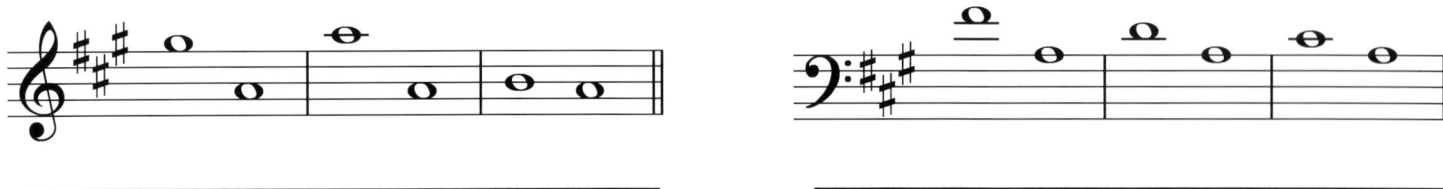

_____   _____

Quick Quiz

1. **Above** each note write a **higher** note to form the named **harmonic** interval. /6
   The key is B♭ major. (Watch out when you write a 2nd – it's the only one that won't be 'above'.)

   5th   8ve   3rd   7th   2nd   4th

2. Write the scale degrees under the notes marked with * for this E minor melody. /6

   1st ___   ___   ___   ___   ___   ___

3. Name these notes. To which key do they all belong? _____ /7

   ___   ___   ___   ___   ___

4. Write the scale of D minor descending in the bass clef, in semibreves, /4
   without key signature but with accidentals.

   Which form have you used?

   _____

5. Name two important ingredients in macaroni cheese. /2

   _____ and _____

   Total: /25

Tonic Triads

As you know from Grade 1, a 'tonic triad' is a chord of three notes built on the 'tonic' (scale degree number 1).

Complete the rest of these tonic triads, which are in all the new keys for Grade 2.

When naming the key of a tonic triad, you need to check three things:

1. The bottom note of the triad (also known as the 'root')
2. The key signature (if given)
3. Accidentals (if given)

Now you can go back and name all the tonic triads above! Then name the key of these:

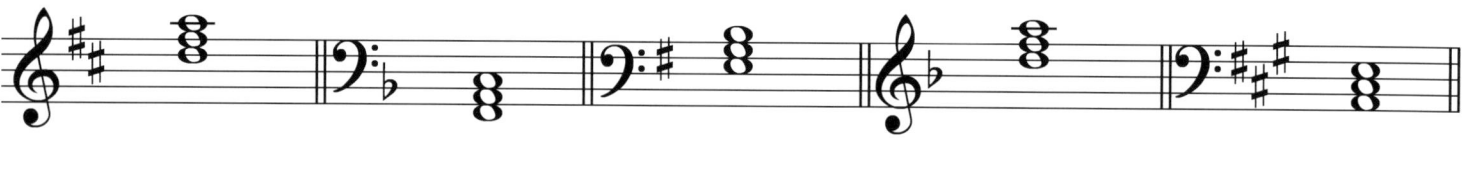

Sometimes tonic triads are written with accidentals instead of key signatures. Watch out for the difference between major and minor:

And check this out... the tonic triads for our two new flat keys look quite different when written with accidentals!

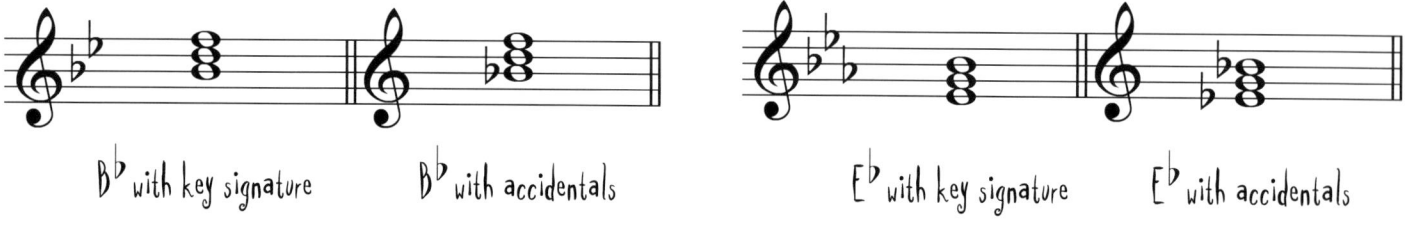

Terrific Triads

1. Name these tonic triads. Remember, check the bottom note and look for accidentals!

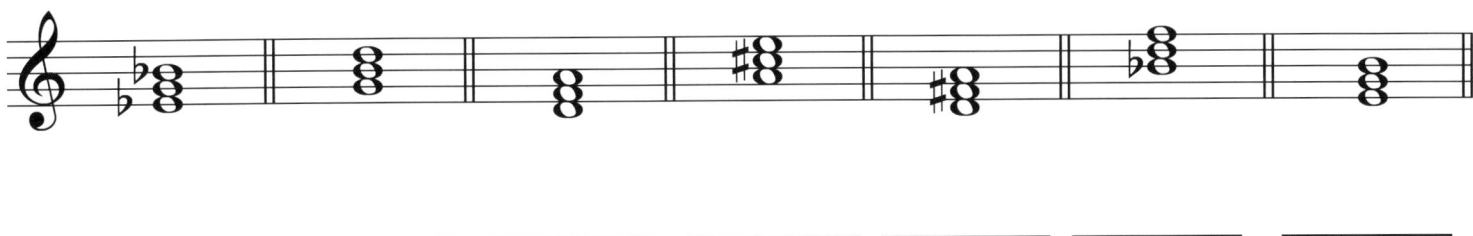

___ ___ ___ ___ ___ ___ ___

2. Write these tonic triads, each with a key signature. Watch out for clef changes!

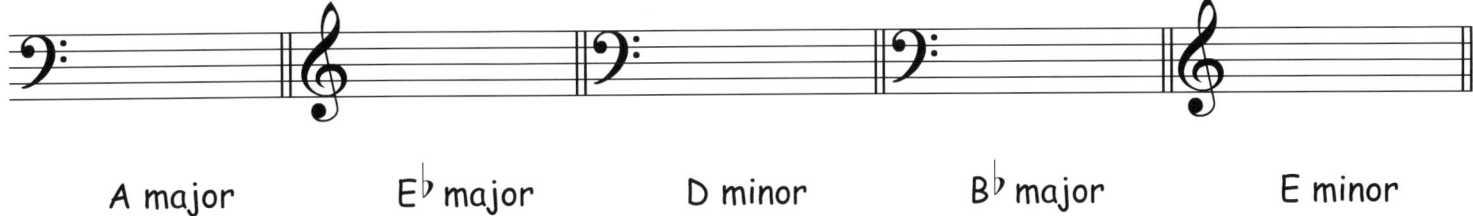

A major   E♭ major   D minor   B♭ major   E minor

3. Write the tonic triads for these MINOR key signatures:

4. Write the following tonic triads with accidentals. (Hint: one of them won't actually need any!)

E♭ major   A major   D major   B♭ major   D minor

Did you check the clef?

5. Name the notes contained in a D major tonic triad: ___ ___ ___

6. Which triad is made up of the notes A, C♯, E? _____

Accidentals → Key Signature

When you convert a melody from accidentals to key signature, the sound will stay exactly the same. It's a simple matter of changing the look of it. For example:

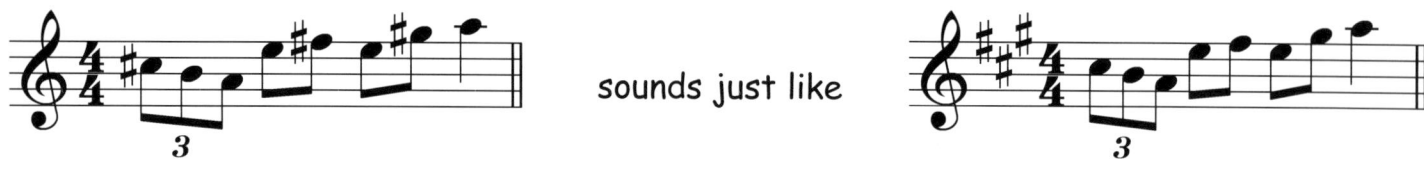

Let's try converting a melody in B♭ major. Here it is, written with accidentals:

1. Cross out all the accidentals relevant to the key signature. In this case, it's all the B flats and E flats – they will 'disappear' into the key signature of B♭ major.

2. Circle all the remaining accidentals – these must be included in your answer (because they are not part of the key signature!).

3. Write the key signature (and time signature) on the stave below and copy the melody, including only the circled accidentals. That's all!

 TOP TIP: In the exam, the first few notes are usually done for you (woo hoo!) but you MUST remember to write the key signature! (You'd be amazed at how many people forget to do this)

Here's another melody. Rewrite it with the key signature of D major. Remember your three steps above!

Key Signature → Accidentals

Great work on the previous page! Now we're going to do it the other way around: converting from key signature to accidentals. Let's try a melody in A major:

1. Write the sharps or flats from the key signature against the relevant notes. In this case, that means find all the Fs, Cs and Gs in the melody and write sharps next to them.

2. Cross out any repetitions of sharps in the **same bar** at that **exact pitch**. (This is because of the rule about accidentals lasting until the next barline — discuss this more with your teacher!)

3. Copy out the melody, including any original accidentals PLUS the sharps you wrote in!

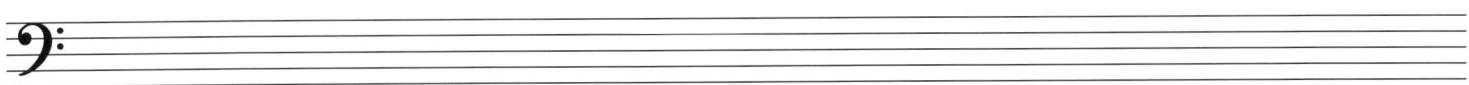

Terrific work! Now rewrite the following melody in E♭ major, without a key signature. Follow the three steps above – especially the bit about including the original accidentals!

Naturals

The only thing to be VERY careful of in these types of questions are the naturals. Naturals can really ruin your day if they occur on notes from the key signature! You have to check **where** they occur in the bar and think about their **function**. Discuss this more with your teacher, and go to **www.blitzbooks.com** for more worksheets on this!

Revision of Everything So Far

1. Rewrite the following melody with the key signature of D major. (Make sure you include any necessary accidentals.)

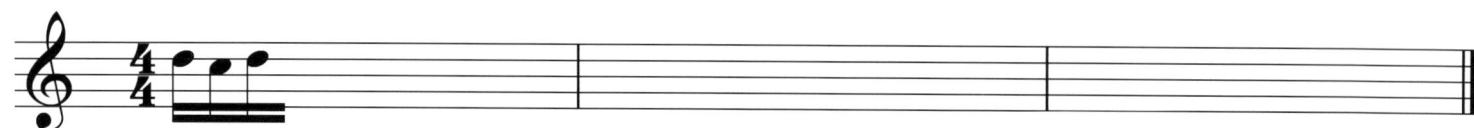

2. Write the tonic triads represented by these major key signatures.

3. At each place marked with an asterisk, add the correct rest/s to complete the bar.

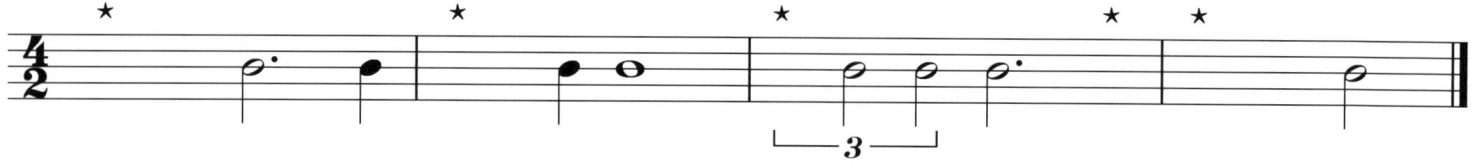

4. Write the equivalent sounding notes, using a different clef. (Make sure you draw the clef!)

5. There are eight errors in the grouping of notes and rests in the melody below. Find them and correct them as you rewrite the whole melody.

6. Name this interval and state whether it is melodic or harmonic: /2

_____

7. Which of these notes does NOT belong to the key of E♭ major? (Circle correct answer) /1

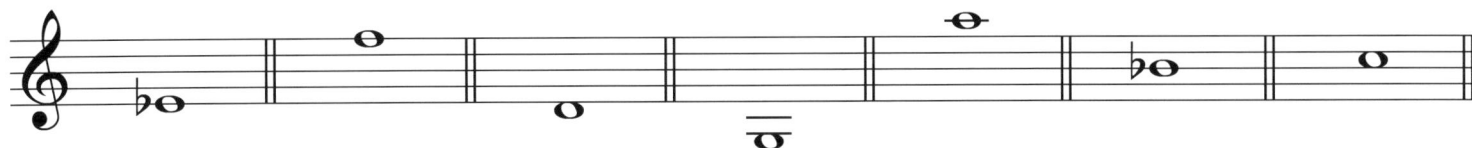

8. What name would have appeared on Darth Vader's birth certificate? /1
(Okay this is not really revision) _____

9. Here is a melody. Follow all the instructions below! /20

★ Add a clef and key signature to make it E minor
★ Find all the 7th scale degrees and raise them by one semitone
★ Draw a rectangle around three consecutive notes that make up the tonic triad
★ Add the missing bar-lines
★ Circle all the intervals of a 4th (melodic intervals, of course... this is a melody!)
★ Add rests in the correct order to complete the final bar
★ Draw a triangle around the shortest note in the melody

10. Check out this note: 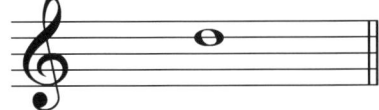 It is the... /2

★ <u>1st</u> scale degree of D major
★ ___ scale degree of B♭ major
★ ___ scale degree of A minor

Total: /62 ← That's a random total, isn't it???

Halving and Doubling

Here are two rhythms for you to clap. Observe the tempo markings. What do you notice?

Adagio

Allegro

That's right, they sound the same, they just look different. See how all the notes in the $\frac{2}{2}$ rhythm are **double** the value of the notes in the $\frac{2}{4}$ rhythm?

In your exam you'll be asked to rewrite a melody with all the notes either halved or doubled. Let's do some quick practice on this by completing the table below.

(Hint: Keep the number of notes in the group the same. For example,  becomes )

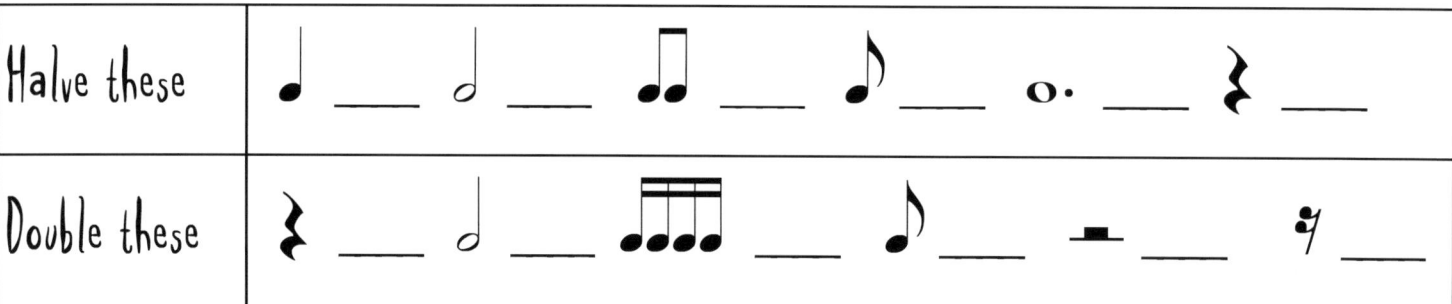

When you halve crotchets into quavers, or quavers into semiquavers, you'll need BEAMS!

So,

If you write the new halved or doubled note values above your given notes, you will then more easily see which notes need to be beamed together.

 **TOP TIP:** When you halve or double the note values you are changing the **bottom** number of the time signature. The top number is not affected at all!

Rewrite these melodies with the notes and rests DOUBLED. Remember, it's helpful to write the new note values above the given melody. The good news is, the new time signature and the first note or two are given to you (yay!).

Fantastic work! And now, rewrite these with the note values HALVED.

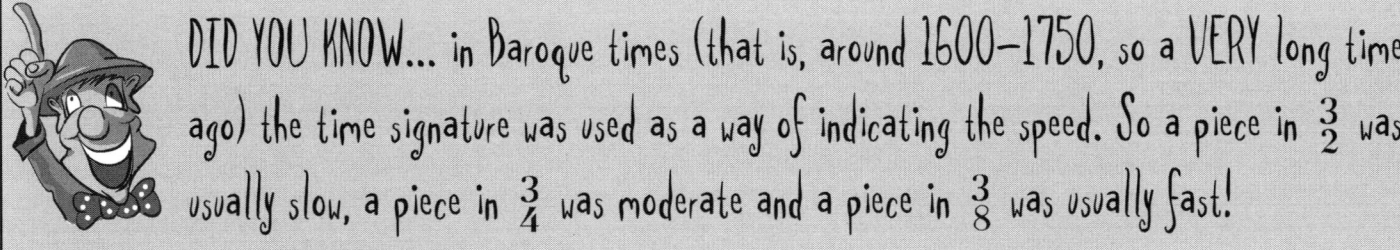

Fix These!

Since grouping is so important when you compose your own rhythms, let's practise it some more. Rewrite these rhythms with the correct grouping in the 'Fix it up' column. The sound of the rhythms must not change, so don't change the order of notes and rests!

Wrong ✗	Why is it wrong?	Fix it up! ✓
	Crotchet rests should be grouped into minim rests	
	Quaver grouping does not show two minim beats	
	Don't beam across 2 and 3 in a group of four semiquavers	
	Rests must be ordered so they complete the beat	
	Must not group 2nd and 3rd minim beats together	
	Quavers and semiquavers should be beamed together	
	Don't beam across 2 and 3 in a group of 4 quavers	
	Beaming must clearly show where a new beat begins	
	Quaver grouping does not show three minim beats	
	Ties should not be used in place of longer note values	

'Time' to Practise (ha ha)

1. Rewrite the following melody showing correct grouping of notes and rests.

2. Now that you have fixed the grouping and beaming above, rewrite the melody once again, using notes and rests that are **twice** the value. (The beginning is done for you, as usual)

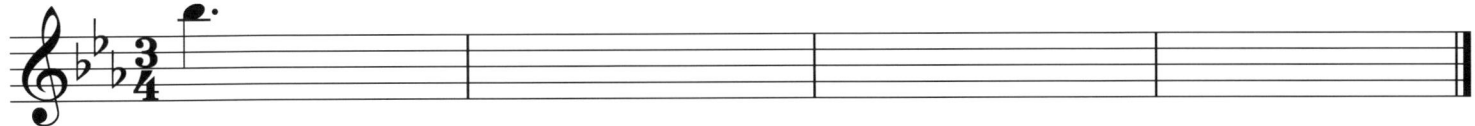

3. Write the correct time signature for each of these two-bar rhythms.

4. At each place marked with an asterisk, add the correct rest/s.

fabulous work!

Switching Clefs

One of the things you have to do in your exam is rewrite a melody in a different clef **without changing the pitch**. We've already done some of this kind of thing (see pages 19 and 42) so this page will be super easy for you.

When switching clefs, leger lines are usually involved.

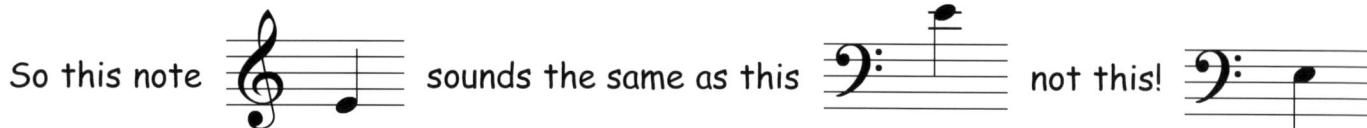

Write the treble notes that would sound exactly the same as these bass notes (remember to adjust the direction of your stems!):

And now do the reverse... write the equivalent treble notes:

OK! So now it's time to try this with a melody. The good news is... in the exam, the first note or two is always done for you!!! How cool is that? You just need to follow the shape and rhythm... and don't forget to adjust your stems!

Rewrite this melody in the bass clef, keeping the pitch the same.

Go to **www.blitzbooks.com** for more FREE theory worksheets!

Timed Test II

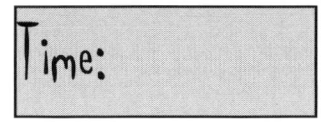

Once again, time yourself doing this quiz. Do it as fast as you can, but remember your teacher will **ADD ON 10 SECONDS** for every mistake. Start the clock!

1. Name this tonic triad:  _____

2. Write the correct time signature for these rhythms:

3. Complete the following bar with semiquavers: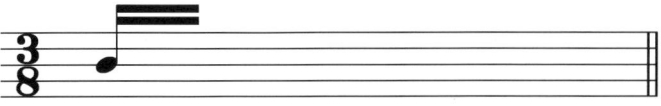

4. Name this interval: 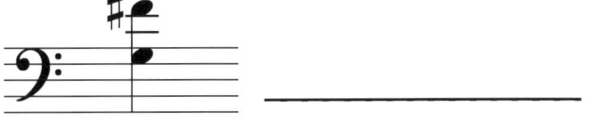 _____

5. Rewrite this short melody with all the note values doubled.

   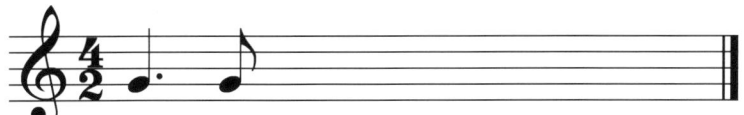

6. Rewrite this short melody in the treble clef, keeping the pitch the same.

   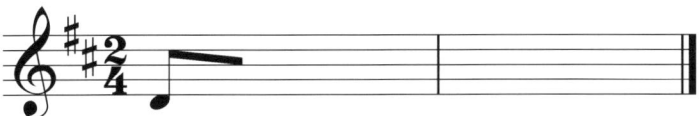

STOP THE CLOCK – FILL IN YOUR TIME AT THE TOP!

☐ I made no mistakes! I keep my time of _____ !

☐ I made _____ mistakes. My new time is _____

Rewrite This!

You're about to rewrite the following melody FOUR times. With each rewrite you'll give it a brand new look! But will anything happen to the sound???

1. Rewrite it with all the notes beamed/grouped correctly.

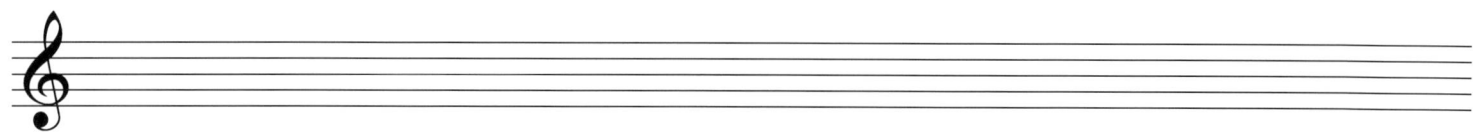

2. Keeping the correct beaming above, rewrite the melody using the key signature of A major. Remember to include any necessary accidentals.

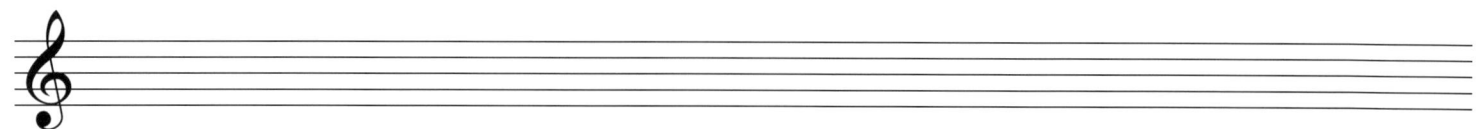

3. Keeping the key signature, rewrite the melody with notes and rests of TWICE the value, using the time signature of $\frac{3}{4}$.

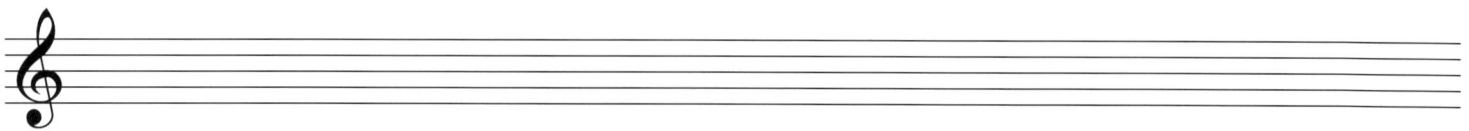

4. Finally, write your 'new-look' $\frac{3}{4}$ melody in the bass clef without changing the pitch!

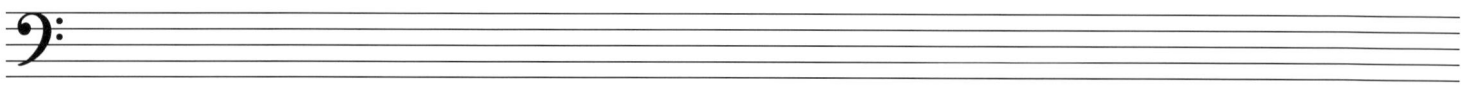

Now go and play all of these melodies on your instrument (unless you play the drums, in which case, don't worry about it). What do you notice about the sound? _____

Box Puzzle

Fill in the answers to the clues below, and find the secret message running down the page... it's what you have to do in harmonic minor scales!!!

1. Three-note chord built on scale degree no. 1. (two words)
2. Major key signature containing two flats.
3. Major keys share their key signatures with the _____ _____ key. (two words)
4. In harmonic minor scales, the 7th note is always _____.
5. $\frac{3}{8}$, $\frac{3}{4}$, and $\frac{3}{2}$ are all examples of _____ _____ time signatures. (two words)
6. Type of minor scale that is not melodic or harmonic.
7. The key signature of A major contains ____ _____ . (two words)
8. Half a crotchet.
9. Italian term meaning moderately short and detached. (See p. 55!)
10. Single note that would fill an entire bar of $\frac{3}{2}$.
11. Symbol that indicates half a bar of silence in $\frac{4}{2}$ time.
12. G♯ is the _____ scale degree of A major.
13. 42 + 51 = ? (two words)
14. Sharps, flats and naturals used outside the key signature.
15. Leger lines are small lines written either below or _____ _____ _____ . (3 words)

51

Terms and Signs

 There are quite a few more terms to learn for Grade 2 (oh well). The terms listed below are **in addition to** the terms for Grade 1, which you can download from **www.blitzbooks.com**. Also check out **How to Blitz Musical Knowledge!**

allargando	–	becoming broader
andantino	–	literally 'small andante'; slightly faster OR slower than 'andante' (walking pace)
assai	–	very (e.g. 'allegro assai' = very quick)
con	–	with (e.g. 'con grazia' = with grace)
con moto	–	with movement
dolce	–	soft and sweet, sweetly
espressivo (espress.)	–	expressively
forte-piano (**fp**)	–	loud then immediately soft
giocoso	–	playful, merry
grave	–	very slow, solemn
grazioso	–	gracefully
largo	–	broadly, slowly
larghetto	–	rather broadly (i.e. not as slow as 'largo')
maestoso	–	majestically
meno mosso	–	less speed (slower)
molto	–	very (e.g. 'molto espr.' = very expressive)
non troppo	–	not too much
piu mosso	–	more speed (faster)
presto	–	very fast
senza	–	without
sforzando (**sfz** or **sf**)	–	a strong accent, forced
simile (sim.)	–	continue in the same way
sostenuto	–	sustained
tenuto	–	'held'; hold note for its full value/ play with slight pressure
vivace/vivo	–	lively and spirited

Sign	Name of Sign	Meaning of Sign
> (accent mark above note)	accent	play strongly
− (tenuto mark above note)	tenuto	hold for full value of note/play note with a slight pressure
·̄ (dot and line above note)	mezzo-staccato (on one note)	moderately short and detached
slur with dots over notes	mezzo-staccato (on more than one note)	moderately short and detached
^ above / v below	strong accent (also called 'marcato')	play strongly
▼ above / ▲ below	staccatissimo	extremely short and detached

There is some expression and articulation missing from the melody below. Follow the instructions to add all the terms and signs... then play it, or ask someone to play it for you!

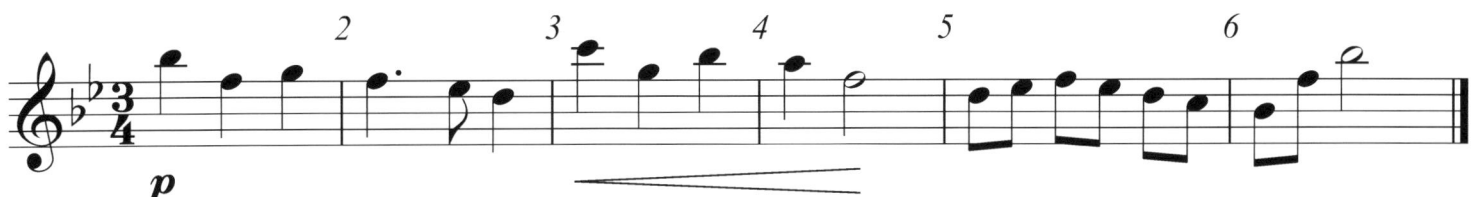

★ Add signs to indicate that the notes in bar 1 are to be played mezzo-staccato.

★ Add a different accent sign to each of the crotchets in bar 3. (Hint: tenuto is a type of accent)

★ Add the abbreviation for a 'forceful accent' to the last note in bar 4.

★ Add an Italian term to show that the melody is to be played rather broadly.

★ Add signs to indicate that the notes in bar 5 should be extremely short and detached.

★ Add an Italian term to show that the melody should be slower in bar 6.

★ Extra challenge: rewrite the melody on the spare manuscript at the back of this book, with all note values halved!

Yet Another Quiz

This quiz includes questions on terms and signs from Grade 1 as well as Grade 2. Make sure you go to **www.blitzbooks.com** for a complete list of terms and signs!

1. Explain '*8va*': _____

2. Write the Italian **abbreviation** that means loud then immediately soft: _____

3. The definition of a triplet is _____

4. What does '*tenuto*' mean? _____

5. Write five Italian terms for tempo in order from slowest to fastest:

   _____ _____ _____ _____ _____
   slowly   at a walking pace   moderately fast   lively and spirited   very fast

6. Explain M.M. ♩ = 60 _____

7. Give the Italian and English meaning of *sfz* : _____

8. Add a mezzo-staccato sign to this note:

9. What does '*staccatissimo*' mean? _____ Draw it here:

10. Translate the Italian words in this sentence: The boy was *molto giocoso* after he ate his chocolate with *piu mosso* than his mother had ever seen. '*Non troppo!*', she told him!

11. True or false: '*andantino*' can be interpreted as slower OR faster than *andante*. _____

12. Explain the difference between *largo* and *larghetto* _____

Use Your Skills

The final question in your exam paper is always centred around a melody, about which you have to answer questions. The next three pages will really prepare you for this! All you need to do is apply all the knowledge and skills you've learned so far in this book.

You will also have a 'copying' question just like you did in Grade 1. This is to assess the neatness of your music handwriting, as well as how well you observe details in the music. Read the question carefully: you may be asked to copy a specific part of the melody, for example 'copy from bar 5 to the end of bar 9'. You do not have to write the bar numbers.

Here we go with the first melody, by Haydn. Study it, then answer the questions below.

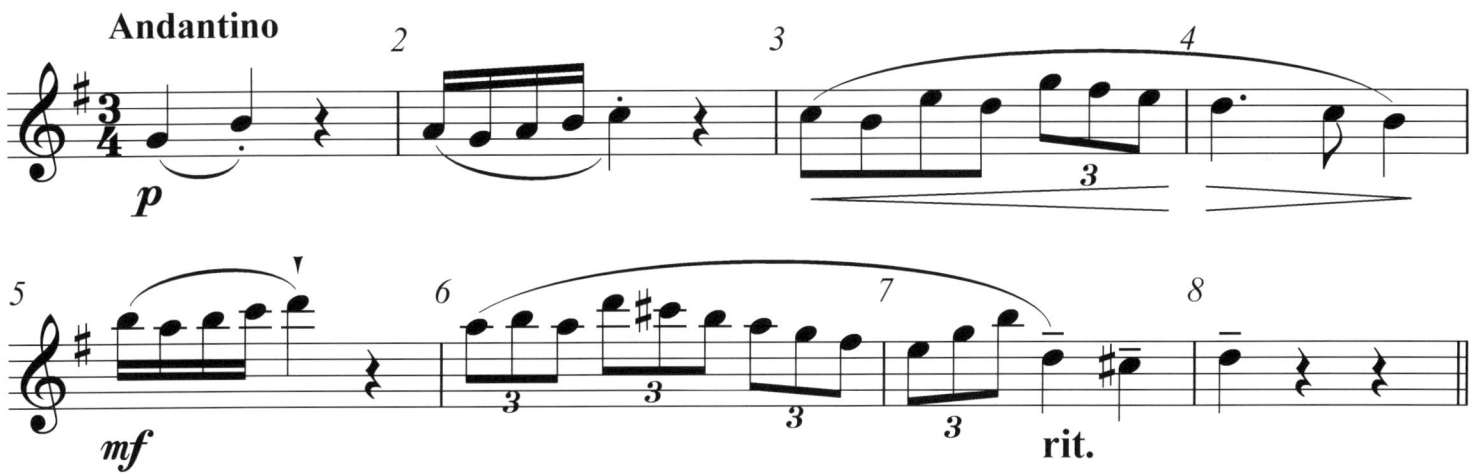

★ What does '*p*' stand for and what does it mean? _____

★ True or false: The melody gets slower at the end. _____

★ This melody begins on the tonic. Name the key. _____

★ Which two bars contain notes that do not belong to this key? _____

★ How many bars contain triplets? _____

★ Circle the highest note of the melody. Which scale degree is this? _____

On the staff below, copy the melody from the beginning of bar 5 to the end of bar 8. Remember to include every tiny detail!

55

Here is the opening of Invention No. 8 by J.S. Bach. Answer the questions below.

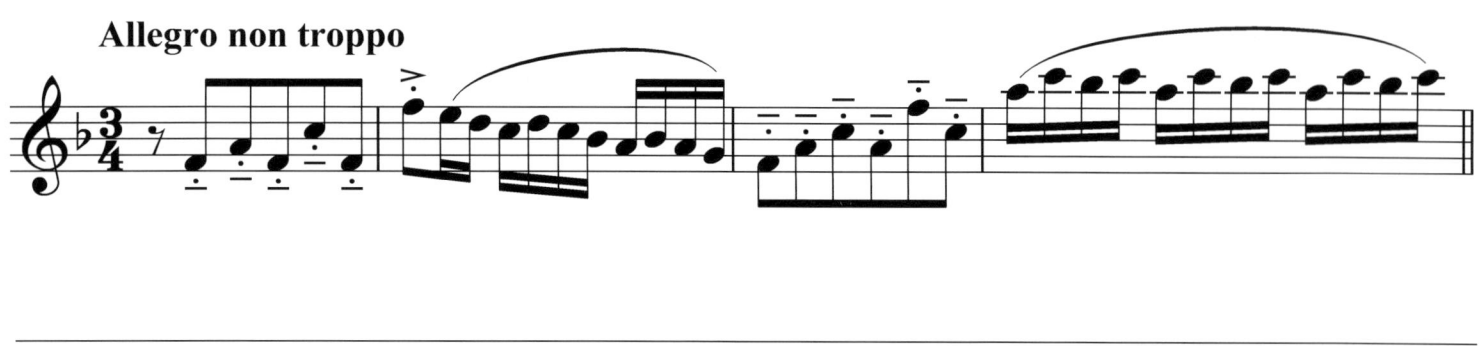

★ At what speed is this music to be played? _____

★ Name and explain the sign on each quaver in bars 1 and 3. _____

_____

★ True or false: This melody is in F major. _____

★ Place a square bracket over three consecutive notes that form the tonic triad.

★ What is the name and value of the rest in bar 1? _____

★ On the staff given above, copy bars 1 and 2 only. Make sure you include the tempo marking.

Great work! Now here is a melody from a sonata by Gurlitt.

★ What does 'Grazioso' mean? _____

★ What does '*sfz*' mean? _____

★ In which bar is the performer told to change tempo? _____ Explain the meaning of the Italian terms indicating this. _____

★ How many bars contain the same rhythm? _____

★ Explain the time signature. _____

On the staff below, copy the Gurlitt melody from the beginning to the end of bar 4.

Here is one more extract, from a sonatina by Kuhlau.

★ How many ties are in this melody? _____ How many slurs? _____

★ How many crotchet beats will the first note of bar 2 sound for? _____

★ Circle a note that does NOT belong to the key of the piece.

★ Explain the signs over the minims in bar 1. _____

★ What does 'Presto' mean? _____

★ How many bars contain nothing but quavers? _____

On the staff above, copy the music from bar 3 to the third beat of bar 6. Draw the clef.

Word Search

←——————→

The answers to the clues on the opposite page are hidden in this grid! The words could be forwards, backwards, horizontal, vertical or diagonal. If you spot a word easily, see if you can match it up with the correct clue!

T	V	G	L	M	S	T	A	C	C	A	T	O
E	I	R	R	A	S	M	E	E	C	L	O	D
H	V	A	R	J	T	A	O	J	L	T	F	N
C	O	V	P	O	U	N	D	T	R	P	L	A
T	S	E	R	R	A	B	E	L	O	H	W	Z
O	C	T	T	T	E	E	J	D	E	R	T	R
R	A	E	R	H	I	L	T	Y	I	E	B	O
C	S	R	F	I	N	R	A	R	R	C	A	F
D	I	L	T	R	P	N	T	T	A	E	C	S
E	L	P	U	D	E	L	P	M	I	S	V	A
T	N	E	C	C	A	P	E	I	S	V	R	R
T	M	E	L	O	D	I	C	T	E	D	E	C
O	E	M	F	O	R	T	E	P	I	A	N	O
D	A	I	R	T	C	I	N	O	T	R	D	N

Go to **www.blitzbooks.com** for FREE worksheets, games, flashcards, manuscript and MORE!

Clues

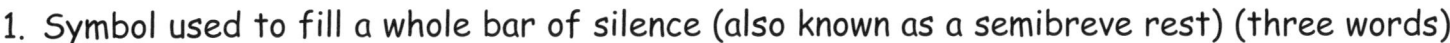

1. Symbol used to fill a whole bar of silence (also known as a semibreve rest) (three words)

2. Italian term for 'loud then immediately soft'

3. Italian term represented by the abbreviation 'sfz'

4. The time signatures 2/2 and 2/4 are examples of _____ _____ time (two words)

5. Name of this interval:

6. This sign means mezzo _____

7. In harmonic minor scales you must _____ the 7th note

8. Name of this sign:

9. Italian term for 'soft and sweet'

10. A single note worth six semiquavers (two words) (hint: there is a dot involved)

11. Two-letter abbreviation for clue no. 2

12. Italian term meaning 'movement' or 'motion' (often seen with the word 'con' before it)

13. E minor is the _____ minor of G major

14. Italian term meaning lively and spirited (four letters)

15. You must raise the 7th in minor scales with an _____

16. The Italian word meaning 'with' that was mentioned in clue no. 12

17. Bart's sister's first name (yes, Bart Simpson)

18. Name of this sign:

19. Intervals that are written side by side are called _____ intervals

20. English translation of 'molto'

21. Italian term meaning very slow and solemn

22. Chord built on scale degree no.1. (two words)

The Absolute Final Revision Test

1. Rewrite this melody with correct grouping/beaming of the notes. /10

2. Circle two consecutive notes that make an interval of an 8ve. /1

3. Name the key of the melody: _____ /1

4. Name another key with the same key signature: _____ /1

5. Turn back to page 53 and study the melody, which has had lots of terms and signs added to it (by you, when you did that page, hopefully). Copy it out here! /10

6. Add the correct clef and accidentals to make this the scale of E minor. /5

Which form of the minor scale have you written above? _____

7. Add the missing clef, key signature and time signature to this melody in A major. /8
   Then add the missing rests at each place marked *.

8. How many semiquaver rests are there in a crotchet rest? _____ /1

9. Just for fun, name the capital of France: _____ /1

10. Write three different time signatures for simple triple time. /6
    Then write a single note that would fill each bar.

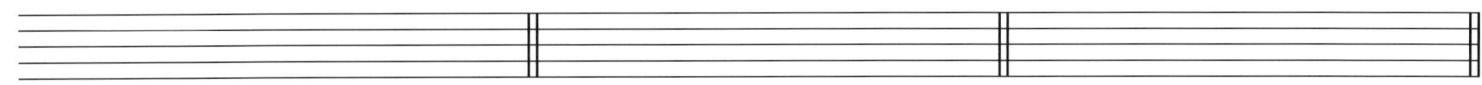

11. Rewrite these bass-clef notes in the treble clef, keeping the pitch the same. /5

12. In which major key are all of these notes found? _____ /1

Total: /50

Mad Multiple Choice

1. In harmonic minor scales, we must

    A. raise the 6th and 7th notes
    B. raise the 7th note
    C. raise all of the notes

2. When deciding the key of a melody, it is important to

    A. look at the key signature
    B. look at the last note
    C. check for accidentals
    D. check which clef it is written in
    E. all of the above

3. The definition of a triplet is:

    A. Two notes played in the time of three notes of equal value
    B. Three notes of equal value played at once
    C. Three notes played in the time of two notes of equal value

4. In $\frac{3}{8}$ time, all the quaver beats should be

    A. beamed together
    B. kept completely separate
    C. friends

5.

    A. 37
    B. $8\frac{1}{2}$
    C. $9\frac{1}{4}$

6. This sign: ▬ fills a bar with silence in

    A. $\frac{4}{2}$ only

    B. $\frac{2}{4}$ only

    C. all time signatures except $\frac{4}{2}$

7. In Grade 2 we have to learn

    A. more Italian terms than in Grade 1

    B. fewer Italian terms than in Grade 1

    C. no Italian terms

8. Circle the correct sign for 'mezzo-staccato' on one note:

    A.    B.   C.

9. When composing a rhythm, we should try to:

    A. use crotchets and minims ONLY

    B. have a good balance of contrast and repetition

    C. make every bar as complicated as possible

10. Accidentals in music last

    A. all through the piece

    B. until the next bar-line

    C. until the double bar-line

11. Melodic minor scales are

    A. major on the way up and natural minor on the way down

    B. annoying

    C. natural minor on the way down

12. The relative of F major is

        A. E minor

        B. G minor

        C. D minor

13. Accent signs look like a miniature

    A. decrescendo sign   B. crescendo sign   C. triangle

14. When rewriting melodies in different clefs, you should

        A. follow the shape

        B. adjust the stems

        C. double check the first note is in the correct position

        D. all of the above

15. The whole-bar rest hangs from

        A. the second line

        B. the third line

        C. the fourth line

16. We must raise the 6th and 7th note in

        A. melodic minor scales ascending only

        B. harmonic minor scales ascending and descending

        C. melodic minor scales ascending and descending

17. Never group quavers in fours if

        A. they are at the beginning of the bar

        B. they cross over two different minim beats

        C. they don't like each other

Test Paper... sort of

All theory books end with a test paper, but this one is DIFFERENT. It already has the answers in it (mostly wrong answers!) and your job is to be the teacher – you have to **mark** it.

When you've found all the mistakes, go to **www.blitzbooks.com** and download the EXACT SAME PAPER – this time with no answers already in it. See if you can get 100%!

★★★★★★★

Theory Paper Grade 2

Time allowed: 1.5 hours

TOTAL MARKS 100

1\. Add the missing bar-lines to these two melodies.
   The first bar-line is given in each.

10

2\. Add the time signature to each of these five examples.

10

3 a) Name the degree of the scale (e.g. 2nd, 3rd) of each of the notes marked *, as shown in the first answer. The key is A major.

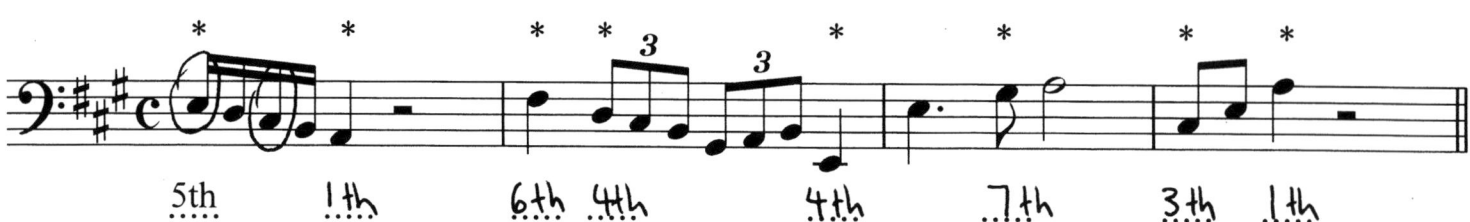

5th   1th   6th 4th   4th   7th   3th 1th

b) Complete this sentence: Each triplet in bar 2 means three quavers (eighth notes) in the time of ...a beat..........

c) Draw a circle around two notes next to each other that are a 3rd apart.

4 Add the correct rest/s at each place marked * to complete the bar.

5 Rewrite this melody in the bass clef, keeping the pitch the same.
The first two notes are given.

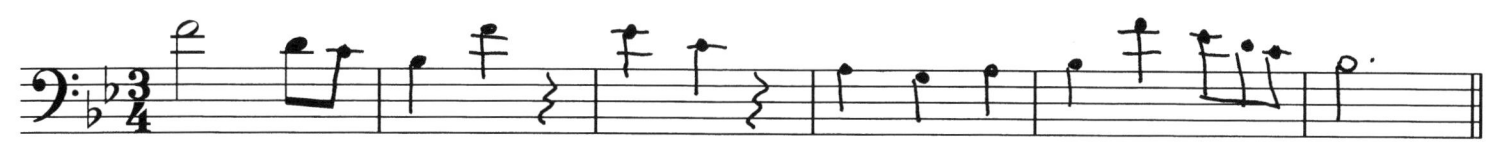

6 Write as semibreves (whole notes) the scales named below.

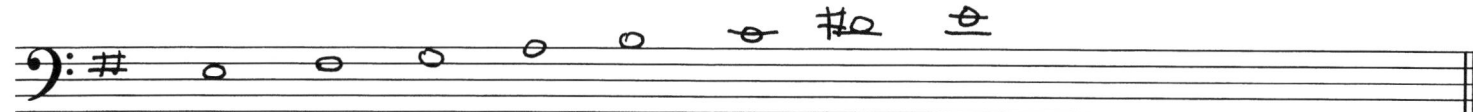

E minor, ascending, with key signature.

Which form of the minor scale have you used? __Melodic I think__

A major, descending, without key signature but adding any necessary sharp or flat signs.

7 Write the following tonic triads with the correct key signature.

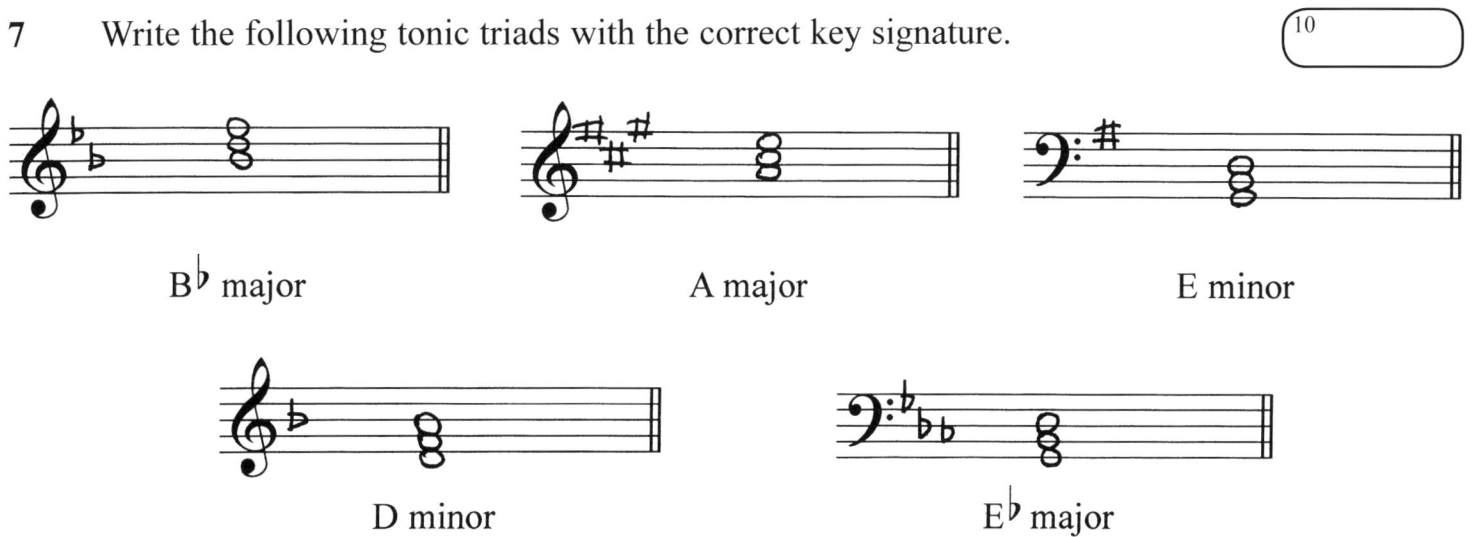

8 Tick one box for each term/sign, as shown in the first answer. (10)

sostenuto means:
- play with slight pressure ☐
- sustained ✓
- strong accent ☐
- very slow, solemn ☐

meno mosso means:
- with movement ☐
- becoming broader ☐
- less speed, slower ✓
- more speed, faster ☐

presto means:
- very fast ✓
- expressively ☐
- playful, merry ☐
- not too much ☐

[symbol] means:
- heavily accented ✓
- hold for full time value ☐
- marcato ☐
- extremely short and detached ☐

sforzando means:
- lively, spirited ☐
- strong accent, forced ✓
- sustained ☐
- short, detached ☐

[triplet symbol] means:
- three quavers, slurred ☐
- three quavers in the time of two crotchets ☐
- three crotchets in the time of two crotchets ☐
- three quavers in the time of two quavers ✓

9   Look at this melody by Clementi and then answer the questions below.

Write your answer to question c) on the stave below.

a)   Give the meaning of:

   (i)   **Vivace** ......Lively and spirited......

   (ii) ∧ (e.g. bars 1 and 2) ......accent......

   (iii) > (e.g. bars 5 and 6) ......accent......

   (iv) The '4' in ¾ ......is the bottom number......

   (v)   The flat sign at the beginning ......is the key signature......

b)   (i)   Which bars contain notes NOT belonging to F major? ......4 + 7......

   (ii) How should the quavers in bar 3 be played? ......As nice as possible......

   (iii) Which bars contain the same rhythm? ......5 + 6......

   (iv) True or false: the entire melody is to be played at the same volume. ......Yep......

   (v)   Find and circle three consecutive notes that make up the tonic triad.

c)   Copy out the first four bars of the melody, exactly as it is written above.
     Don't forget the clef, key signature and all other details. Write the music on the
     blank stave above question a). Marks will be given for neatness and accuracy.

 How did you go marking this paper? Did you find lots of mistakes? Now go to www.blitzbooks.com and download the uncompleted version. Good luck!

Manuscript